T0208305

SURVIVING
IN THE
NEW RETAIL
MARKETPLACE

RETHINKING MARKETING
FOR SMALL BUSINESSES

DOUGLAS D. KELLY

BALBOA.
PRESS
A DIVISION OF HAY HOUSE

Balboa Press books may be ordered through booksellers or by contacting:

Balboa Press
A Division of Hay House
1663 Liberty Drive
Bloomington, IN 47403
www.balboapress.com
1 (877) 407-4847

Because of the dynamic nature of the Internet, any web addresses or links contained in this book may have changed since publication and may no longer be valid. The views expressed in this work are solely those of the author and do not necessarily reflect the views of the publisher, and the publisher hereby disclaims any responsibility for them.

This book is a work of non-fiction. Unless otherwise noted, the author and the publisher make no explicit guarantees as to the accuracy of the information contained in this book and in some cases, names of people and places have been altered to protect their privacy.

The author of this book does not dispense medical advice or prescribe the use of any technique as a form of treatment for physical, emotional, or medical problems without the advice of a physician, either directly or indirectly. The intent of the author is only to offer information of a general nature to help you in your quest for emotional and spiritual well-being. In the event you use any of the information in this book for yourself, which is your constitutional right, the author and the publisher assume no responsibility for your actions.

Any people depicted in stock imagery provided by Getty Images are models, and such images are being used for illustrative purposes only.
Certain stock imagery © Getty Images.

Print information available on the last page.

ISBN: 978-1-9822-3101-9 (sc)
ISBN: 978-1-9822-3100-2 (hc)
ISBN: 978-1-9822-3102-6 (e)

Library of Congress Control Number: 2019909448

Balboa Press rev. date: 07/23/2019

THE NEW RETAIL PARADIGM

THE RETAIL MARKETPLACE HAS UNDERGONE AN ALMOST MIND-BOGGLING CHANGE IN THE WAY IT FUNCTIONS.

Retail businesses are experiencing the greatest shift in their business paradigm in more than sixty years.

Online shopping has become the defining force of retail because it enables prospects and customers to have more choices than ever before. It presently accounts for about seventy percent of all retail sales. The effect of this is that the retail marketplace is now consumer oriented.

A new kind of consumer has emerged with a very different way of making buying decisions. These new consumers are much pickier and more selective because they know they aren't limited to conventional ways of shopping.

Perceptions of companies and their products held by consumers are the only things that matter. This means that increased sales are only achieved if you understand your prospects' and customers' perceptions of both your product and your company.

Marketers must realize that these new consumers want to feel engaged with your business on an emotional level. They aren't interested in one-off transactions with conventional retailers.

Numerous credible studies of these consumers find that they believe traditional retailers, local stores, and certainly big-name retailers found in shopping malls have taken them for granted and provided them with less customer service because the retailers know the consumers have few other options.

This has been the kiss of death for traditional retailers, and many are learning this the hard way.

You've undoubtedly noticed that major stores are going broke; shopping malls have been in deep financial trouble, some even vacant or nearly vacant. This is not limited to certain regions of the country. They're closing everywhere throughout the nation. You can see this for yourself.

The reason is that they haven't recognized that a new marketplace is overtaking them. And they don't realize how fast this new marketplace is moving.

Yet sales of discretionary products—furniture, home electronics, vehicles, even housing—are growing rapidly. Why is this?

It's because businesses selling these products know that their products require a larger expenditure and are not purchased impulsively. To make a sale they must build relationships with their prospects and customers. Relationships begin with empathy and understanding on an emotional level.

Astute marketers work hard to create relationships with all their customers because human nature tells us that people desire relationships not just transactions.

Many things may change, but people will always seek relationships and do business with people and companies they like. This book is about why they like certain businesses and not others. It's about people as consumers.

I can almost guarantee that after reading this book you'll never see the world the same way again.

Douglas D. Kelly
April 17, 2019

RETHINKING MARKETING FOR SMALL BUSINESSES

This book is for owners, operators, managers, salespeople, employees, investors, and any others who have a stake in the outcome of a business that must operate in this new retail marketplace.

Small businesses operate with a very different business model than large businesses. The differences in business models become very apparent in this book as we analyze marketing for your business compared to the ways that big businesses must market products and services.

❧❧

A small business is any business employing fewer than five hundred people. There are 30.2 million small businesses registered in the United States, compared to just 18,500 companies of five hundred employees or more — those which constitute big business—according to government definitions.

That means almost half of the nation's private sector workforce (47.5 percent) are employed by small businesses. Small businesses created 1.9 million net new jobs during 2015[1], the latest year shown by government statistics.

Firms employing fewer than 20 employees experienced the largest gains, adding 1.1 million net jobs.

Since 1995, small businesses have been responsible for creating two out of every three net new jobs in our country, accounting for 47.5 percent of US payroll dollars in 2015, according to the most recent survey available (Source: SUSB).

That's huge. As a small business, your company is part of a major force driving our economy in job creation and payroll.

---

[1] Source: SUSB an annual series that provides national and subnational data on the distribution of economic data by enterprise size and industry.

PREFACE

You who have the courage and perseverance to operate a business, start up a new business, or reinvent a company have my undying admiration. You're the strivers in the world. Without people like you, we'd still be farming with wooden sticks.

In the years since 2008, retail marketing and sales have undergone an extraordinary change. Consumer expectations have also changed extraordinarily. So, the fundamental organic nature of retail marketing has also changed.[2]

But I know you'll continue to strive no matter what.

It's who you are.

This book is an information tool for getting and keeping customers in this new retail marketplace. You'll be guided to develop a good-to-great marketing plan, a good-to-great advertising plan, and ultimately more effective ways of making sales exceeding your present expectations.

You'll learn that you can go up against any competitor, large or small, because you'll come to understand your prospects and customers better than your competitors. And so, you'll know how to sell your product or service better. Be confident of that.

Once upon a time, companies could create customers and drive outcomes through product and price, but that time has passed. The new consumer is savvier and more difficult to please. And they also care a great deal about the quality of their buying experience — something new for many marketers.

---

[2] It's estimated that by 2020, customers will manage 85 percent of his/her relationship with an enterprise without interacting with a single human. Amazon.com's success is the best example of this.

SURVIVING IN THE NEW RETAIL MARKETPLACE

FOR MOST SMALL BUSINESSES, THE WOLF IS ALWAYS AT THE DOOR

I've written this book for small businesses and the people who run them. Your business needs the same knowledge that big businesses need. But it's well known that small businesses handle it better because there's no room for slippage in operating a small business.

Operating a business is stressful because everything is up close. You must deal with problems and find solutions. So, in most small businesses, the wolf is always at the door.

Big businesses have the resources (not always used well) to do many big things, but their business model is much different. So, you'll discover how and why big businesses make some of the most spectacular mistakes because of groupthink — a trap of their own making.

The big takeaway from this book is that your business has nothing to fear from big businesses when you're confronted by them as your competition, because you operate under a different set of rules. You can move more quickly. You're more agile, and your methods and policies can be much more flexible.

But mainly it's because after reading this book, you'll have a deep, pragmatic understanding of how to get and keep customers.

That's the only purpose of a business. Yet it's the thing that most businesses, big and small, get wrong.

The present paradigm shift can be critical and threatening. It has permanently changed the way marketers must respond to their marketplace and the way businesses must now operate.

In 2016, more publicly owned companies went broke than in any other year in history. But that record was broken in 2017, when even more companies went out of business. It appears that this year will be no different. This is startling but not surprising.

There are several reasons for this, but the major reason is that most big businesses have defined their customers by the products they buy; these businesses were and are product driven.

But that era has passed. The new marketplace is not product driven anymore. Now it's defined and driven by the consumer—a new kind of consumer with a wide variety of options.

Consumers buy from business that serve them the best. This may seem obvious, but it makes a big difference in how you must operate in response to this new marketplace.

These new consumers want a relationship with dependable companies they can trust. And to that end, consumers are abandoning businesses that only offer transactions.

If your company doesn't offer a relationship with consumers, they'll leave you to find one that does. I promise you that.

Think about this deeply.

The world is your oyster if you can offer the consumer a relationship with empathy.

KEEP YOUR EYE ON THE BALL, YOUR SHOULDER TO THE WHEEL, AND YOUR NOSE TO THE GRINDSTONE

NOW TRY TO WORK IN THAT POSITION

When I began my career in marketing, I had much to learn. I knew so little that I didn't even know what I didn't know.

I marveled at the seasoned veterans in the big-time advertising agency where I began. It seemed to me I was watching oracles at work.

It was as if they'd been born into the world fully versed in marketing the way IBM representatives seem to have been born in three-piece suits.

I worked hard and began to learn a lot of things. But the more I worked at it, the more I realized I didn't know.

My first aha moment was when I learned that the most important thing in marketing is understanding the perceptions of your product held by your prospects in your marketplace. That means understanding how prospects understand your product personally.

This was a profound realization because I learned that the true effort in acquiring customers isn't about the actual product. It's about the prospect's perception of the product.

The first thing I learned is that a marketer is shooting in the dark if he or she doesn't understand the perceptions held by prospects and customers of the marketer's product.

I work with clients daily to help solve their marketing and advertising problems to reach their sales objectives. So, I'm intensely involved in the same marketplace as you and your business. And I want to help you know what I've come to know after nearly thirty-five years of operating a midsize advertising agency.

You may think that if I operated a large advertising agency, like the agency where I began, I could dazzle you with astounding new ideas and concepts. But that would mischaracterize my purpose here.

Operating a midsize advertising agency allowed me to be a part of the whole process of marketing and advertising and even to work with clients' sales. This enables me to help you understand the elements of marketing and advertising close up because I've been involved in it close up.

In this book, I refer to the experiences and knowledge I've gained from real-world experience. I won't waste your time with theoreticals, hypotheticals, or business school jargon. We're working in the real world, where there are real-world consequences to what we do.

There have been a lot of changes and twists and turns in marketing, advertising, and selling throughout the years. But believe me when I tell you that this new marketplace is different from any before it.

It's a paradigm change that's here to stay. And it's moving very fast, with innovations that are certainly not traditional.

A new kind of consumer is afoot, and this consumer's attitude is different to the point of changing the way marketers must respond. It's serious stuff.

> ## LET US TALK OF MANY THINGS OF SHOES—AND SHIPS—AND SEALING-WAX — OF CABBAGES—AND KINGS — AND HOW MARKETING IS A PLETHORA OF MANY, MANY THINGS.

I don't believe it's possible to know too much. So, we must understand marketing as a continuing journey revealing new ways of seeing the familiar as well as the unfamiliar.

And we must discover new ideas. Nothing is more powerful than an idea.

Ideas can change the world.

This is a good time to let you in on a not-so-well-kept secret. Many of those who write about marketing, or who teach marketing, seldom offer new ideas or go beyond conventional thinking. That is, they seldom go off the beaten path. Some do, but not many.

The fact is most people are instinctively afraid of the path less traveled. Fear drives an emotional need for safety, so most prefer to remain safely on the beaten path.

But fear causes timidity. It locks up the mind and kills the imagination, the most wondrous capability of your mind.

But worse, the beaten path is the conventional path, and it only leads to conventional thinking. And that, in turn, only leads to conventional ideas.

You see, conventional thinking will get you nowhere in the fast-moving, overstimulated marketplace of today. It may even pull you backward.

---

[3] With due respect to Lewis Carroll's "The Walrus and the Carpenter"

Lack of imagination and failure to accept new ideas are the chief reasons many businesses fail.

So, we're going off the beaten path. We'll rethink marketing to discover what our new, fast-paced marketplace is about and how you can make your own path with confidence and meet it on your terms.

Creating a product to fill a market need is what marketing is about. But there's more to it. For a product to be successful, it must meet and fulfill an emotional need of your prospect. If a product can fulfill more than one emotional need, then that's even better because everything in the human sphere is about emotions.

Emotional needs drive all decisions, so you must cause prospects to feel an emotional need for your product or service. To express an emotional need effectively, empathy must be a part of your message.

This matters more than any other single thing; more than your offer, more than the price, and more than a list of benefits.

Many good, hardworking marketers fail because they don't understand emotional needs and the need to empathize. But it's an absolute necessity in our customer-oriented marketplace.

Consider a marketer's website. A lot of website owners are puzzled because their websites don't seem to be working as well as others that are measured the same way. Fewer clicks. Almost always it's because no emotions are associated with it by visitors. Of course, other reasons may be that it's poorly written, has no visual appeal, or may not be relevant to the viewer.

But we're evaluating the importance of emotions; they have everything to do with reaching people with empathy and creating engagement.

Yet many websites show no emotion and, therefore, no understanding of the customer. These websites are simply not customer oriented because a mistaken idea persists that online customers are only looking for products or services and nothing else. The result is the viewer will pause for a moment (4 seconds is the average amount of time), then they will leave your website in search of something better – something that draws them in emotionally.

To have a hardworking website in the new marketplace, your prospects' and customers' emotional needs are the most important things you must grasp and use to reach them.

As you come to understand this, you'll soon know why some of your competitors are succeeding and why some are failing.

IT IS NOT THE STRONGEST OF THE SPECIES, NOR THE MOST INTELLIGENT THAT SURVIVES.

IT'S THE ONE THAT IS THE MOST ADAPTABLE TO CHANGE.
—An idea suggested by Charles Darwin

Here is a short list of concepts derived from this. Think about these deeply. They will help you get and keep customers:

- There are foundational elements of marketing that never vary.
- The marketplace is organic. It's dynamic, so it's constantly changing, acting, and reacting to pressures and influences as if it's a living thing.
- The marketplace is people and their emotional needs. The pressures and influences on the organic marketplace are the people's needs and the marketers' offerings.
- The organic marketplace operates on clear principles. I call them *natural laws.* They bind and affect every marketer in the same ways. No one gets a pass. Yet most marketers aren't even aware of them.
- Understanding the organic marketplace in depth will reveal actions and reactions that will directly improve your marketing.
- The path we'll take follows the organic nature of the marketplace. And it's not linear.
- Many marketers are overwhelmed by the marketplace because they underestimate its depth. We'll clearly identify the new marketplace and understand its forces, so you won't be overwhelmed.
- You'll find you can successfully pit your business against any competitor and win if you can free yourself from the ways you've been conditioned to think about your products and services, and about your prospects and customers.

- Getting new customers has changed a lot in our new fast-paced marketplace. You'll have an advantage since it's not difficult; it only requires new thinking.
- Customers are a business's only real asset. I know from experience that most of your competitors fail to understand this, so it gives you a tremendous advantage.
- As you create a marketing plan, you'll discover the critical issues of your own business and how to address them. They are the most valuable things you can know. I'll show you how.
- You'll find the important elements you'll need to conceive and write an accurate, precise marketing plan that you can follow like a recipe. And this will enable you to develop a bulletproof advertising and sales plan.

Marketing will become a way of thinking. Once you're involved in it, you'll never see the world the same way again.

THERE'LL ALWAYS BE SERENDIPITY INVOLVED IN DISCOVERY

—Jeff Bezos
Amazon.com

If you're like most people with motivation and initiative, you'll get an idea and go with it. Yet you may find that where it takes you is not where you intended to go. So, you'll take your next idea and move in another direction. Don't worry. It's part of the process you must go through to get it right.

Don't be afraid of failure. Failure only means you're striving. If you haven't failed, maybe you ought to be a bit worried. It could mean you haven't tried hard enough.

Bill Gates took the wrong direction in his first business Traf-O-Data, and he failed big time. So, Bill began again in a new direction and ended up doing pretty well. It's always the case. Serendipity happens when you're least expecting it.

A phenomenon known as the "serendipity effect" says that if you're working toward a goal and working hard without the distractions of doubt and negativity, then you'll find what you're searching for almost as if by accident. Some people don't believe in serendipity. But that's only saying they haven't done enough. Serendipity is an ancient law that has created success when only failure seemed in sight.

New ideas and insights lead to different ways of understanding things. You can always learn more. There's no such thing as knowing enough. No one knows that much.

Stay very curious and keep moving, continually exploring new ideas. It's guaranteed that you'll come across new ideas that haven't been apparent. And they'll be what you were looking for all along.

Serendipity.

TEETH-GNASHING ANGST AND EXISTENTIAL THREATS

FIDDLY-DEE, I'LL WORRY ABOUT THAT TOMORROW.
—Scarlett O'Hara
Gone with the Wind (1939)

Marketing requires exploration and discovery. But in exploring new places and things, there are pitfalls: low-hanging branches and vines that whack you in the head before you see them, stones in the road to stumble over.

Be wary, but not afraid. Exploration leads to discovery. It's the only thing that does. Where would we be without Columbus and his search for an ocean passage to India? Okay, we'd be on some island in the Caribbean. But you know what I mean.

Let's talk about some unknown things that can screw up your best-laid plans simply because you didn't know. But worse, you didn't know that you didn't know.

It's apparent Columbus knew one thing. He knew the world was round. But that led him into the weeds, because he didn't know the world was a lot bigger than he'd imagined. And of all things, he didn't know there was a huge landmass to his west between Spain and India.

Well, that sure fouled up his plans.

Columbus was stubborn. So now we have islands in the Caribbean he named the Indies (now the West Indies) for no other reason than Columbus thought he'd landed in India. But we can somewhat excuse him for this. Have you ever seen the maps (charts) navigators and pilots used in the fifteenth century? Holy Santa Maria, they were awful because no one knew anything about what lay beyond the shores of Europe. And he was a long way from the shores of Europe.

Okay, enough of the analogy. Let's get down to it. If you're just starting out in business there's no shame in not knowing some things. But it causes teeth-gnashing angst when you're confronted with a problem and no solution. Maybe you got into the problem because you didn't know what you didn't know. Same as with Columbus. We've all been in that place. So, we just plunge ahead.

One of the reasons I've written this book is to stimulate some self-exploration and objectivity, to refresh your thinking, refresh your interest in yourself and the amazing things the mind can do.

Angst is very overrated. You'll come to know this.

Even if you know a lot or a little about marketing, I'll rid you of angst. Simply opening your mind helps you find new and different ways of using information to create a solid marketing plan.

Once you begin the journey, it becomes easier. And a lot more fun.

If you're in the marketing side of a company, you may improve your existing marketing plan. Maybe I'll remind you of things you may not have considered.

If you have several marketing plans—one for each product line, brand, or marketplace your company serves, then I may spark new ideas and solutions. Learn to think differently, to think bigger and broader.

But then there's this other thing.

After working in the trenches for so long, your thoughts and ideas tend to be focused only on the trench. That means thinking familiar thoughts. The same ideas over and over. Nothing fresh there.

So, you need a new way to approach problems. One that stimulates and refreshes your interest, to bring forth ideas that have been lurking in the back of your mind almost forgotten.

It's easier to find stimulating things when you climb out of the trench and look around. You'll see the horizon from there. You'll see lots of things you hadn't noticed or thought about.

You'll find fresh thinking that naturally comes from having objectivity.

Without objectivity, you'll be working with the same facts and knowledge. And that breeds familiarity. Those familiar thoughts.

Familiarity can be the kiss of death to problem solving.

Familiarity can cause you to overlook the obvious.

We've all done it and realized too late we've become blind to the obvious.

Teeth-gnashing angst is the next thing you experience. But angst isn't healthy. And you'll wear down your teeth.

The next chapter is a perfect example of how familiarity can cause very smart and experienced people to overlook the obvious.

UP JUMPS THE DEVIL

CALL YOUR PRIEST, RABBI, OR SPIRITUAL ADVISOR.
IT HAPPENS WHEN YOU LEAST EXPECT IT.

I've worked with top management people in international, publicly owned companies. These companies have highly qualified people, very smart people in positions of heavy responsibility.

We worked with one such company, a very good company, for years. The people were quite smart and great to work with. You'd recognize the company's name and brand. You probably have its products in your kitchen. They're excellent products too.

Yet three people I worked with there, smart people, should have, could have, would have recognized the cause of a problem that they'd asked me to help them solve if they hadn't been so close to it and paralyzed by fear. Fear can be debilitating. It can freeze up the mind, killing fresh thinking.

I'll admit to being surprised they couldn't see the cause of their problem when we looked at their sales chart. And I wondered if I might already have a glimpse of the problem. But I sat quietly and listened. Anything I might say would sound as though I was trying to be the smartest guy in the room. Never be that guy.

My assignment from them, after a long meeting during which they repeated the same problem in different ways, was to figure out why their sales were so choppy. As their past year's sales chart sat on an easel glaring down at us, it crossed my mind that it looked like a child's drawing of mountains. Zigzag peaks and valleys from side to side of the whole chart. Ah, man.

The VP pointed to the chart and said that they wanted to cut out all the valleys and leave all the peaks. Hah. Imagine that. Of course. Wouldn't that be wonderful? No pressure here.

I considered the usual suspects causing the problem, but I said nothing. I could be wrong. To mix a metaphor, eating crow is not my cup of tea. And it appears to be very unprofessional.

So, I asked them for all their sales information including regular case-lot prices and promotional case-lot prices, each of the sales promotion dates for the past year, and the specific volume purchases from distributors and dates of each purchase. They eagerly ask their people to furnish me everything I'd requested.

Hot damn, the marketing guy might pull this off and figure it out.

I put the information together back at my office, and it was just as I had suspected. They had consistently offered discounts to their distributors at fairly predictable intervals. So, what do you think the distributors did? Right. Just what we'd all do. Hold off buying until the next discounts, then buy everything they could.

The company's sales manager had inadvertently "trained" their distributors when to buy. I doubt this ever occurred to him. He'd merely set an annual calendar for discounts to move inventory and pump up sales.

Never underestimate the tragic results of familiarity. We've just discussed being so close to a thing that the obvious is invisible.

When one delivers not-so-great news like this, one must be humble. Not smug. Smug is insulting and demeaning. Unkind. When I pulled out my stuff, they saw the bad news immediately. These people weren't stupid. But they make mistakes and fail to see the obvious just like everyone else.

We worked out a varying formula that was much less predictable for determining the dates of promotional pricing to move products. And guess what. Their revenues were up the next year. And the valleys caused after promotions were predictable, so they could be offset. I did accomplish what they wanted. And you could have as well.

These companies are big and have more money, which can tide them over through some mistakes. But that can cause a greater problem.

The greater problem is that these companies tend to be insular. The decision-makers are not exposed directly to the results of many of their decisions. And they only talk to each other, which creates groupthink, a dire problem not easily recognized. This is one reason they retained us: to keep them objective.

I told you they were smart.

There are lots of people involved in their business flow. That makes it very difficult to react quickly or react with full knowledge of what's happening when suddenly up jumps the devil.

WE HAVE ONLY AN ILLUSION OF INSIGHT, AN ILLUSION OF UNDERSTANDING

THE SINGLE BIGGEST PROBLEM IN COMMUNICATION
IS THE ILLUSION THAT IT HAS TAKEN PLACE.
—George Bernard Shaw

Communicating to your prospects and customers always requires a personal message because you can't know where they'll be when your message comes to them. They may be in their living rooms, at bars, or driving their cars, riding buses, or some other place outside their usual context. Without considering context, you may only have the illusion that your message has been processed by them no matter what Nielsen ratings show about out-of-home impressions.

You must know for certain that, no matter the environment or distractions, your prospect will receive your communication and understand it.

To cut through the normal everyday clutter of distractions requires you to use a personal message. Yes, a personal message. That means you must use perceptions already in the mind of your prospects and customers.

Those who minimize the importance of their prospects' and customers' perceptions of their product will lose customers and never know why. Their customers will simply go elsewhere because they find another company that understands their needs and communicates to them within their perceptions.

Remember: all advertising is personal. Never communicate as if you're speaking to a group of people. That's impersonal. Cold. Not to mention, it doesn't work.

Pay no attention to the popular term *mass media*. It's a misnomer that implies you're speaking to the masses. You're not but that creates the wrong perception by your prospects and customers, and the wrong impression in your own mind as well.

Messages, communications, and advertising, what one might call "mass media", must always be done as if one is speaking to a single person and that person is the only person seeing it, hearing it, or reading it. I cannot emphasize this enough. It's absolute.

The many points of contact for personal communication are important now more than ever in our new marketplace. They create a symbiotic relationship we'll discuss more in the next chapter.

Don't find yourself with only an illusion of communicating. You'll waste money and time because you'll fail to involve your prospects and customers in your message. And that destroys any engagement you ought to have created.

The single most important thing affecting all marketing and the execution of its strategy all the time, every time, is perceptions. Perceptions are the foundation of marketing.

Perceptions are the force behind the marketplace; the reason the marketplace is organic. Perceptions establish the nature of all marketplaces and the natural laws all marketers are bound by.

Perceptions are the absolute starting point of marketing.

THE MEDIUM YOU USE BECOMES AN INTRINSIC PART OF THE MESSAGE

WHAT YOU'RE ADVERTISING AND TO WHOM DICTATES THE MEDIA USED

The correct medium to reach your market to effectively communicate with your prospects depends entirely on what your objectives are. There's no best medium for everything.

You'll discover the most appropriate medium for your market and for your prospects when you understand where your business best operates in the new marketplace. And more, you'll discover that the medium itself (print, TV, radio, video, smoke signals) is an essential part of your message. Think about that for a moment.

Some fifty years ago, Marshall McLuhan, an innovative thinker, wrote a book, *The Medium Is the Message*. His thesis was (quoting from his book) "the form of a medium embeds itself in any message it would transmit or convey, creating a symbiotic relationship by which the medium influences how the message is perceived."

Effective communication happens when the medium enhances the message. But not all mediums enhance a message.

There's much more to this than one might first realize. The effectiveness of a message depends on the medium used to reach the targeted person. And if it's done well, the medium and the message act together to become the whole of the communication itself.

The best communication in any medium is focused on and directed to the targeted person as an individual. That means it's perceived to be a personal message, and that's the most effective way to convey a message.

PERCEPTION IS REALITY, BUT WHOSE REALITY?

NOTHING IS MORE DECEPTIVE THAN THE OBVIOUS.
—Sherlock Holmes

Each person's perceptions are their individual realities, meaning that everyone does not think alike. Everyone doesn't see the world the same way as you or I. They perceive the world as it fits their beliefs, which is their own reality.

Perceptions of your product or service are what you're selling. And perceptions of your product or service are what your prospects are buying. It's how the mind works. And so, it's the basis of all marketing: the absolute truth underlying all marketing. And more, it's also affected by a person's perception of themselves and their world.

I'm astonished that many people and companies don't know a thing about perceptions. So, they ignore them. Usually, the worst possible thing happens to these companies. By ignoring perceptions, they invariably think they have the best product on the market, so they pay no attention to perceptions or to anything else. They think the best product should be obvious to anyone. So, they try to sell their product as being the best product. Yet saying they have the best product won't make a sale. In fact, it won't even enter the prospect's mind, and here's why.

No one can be told, "This is the best product," with the expectation they'll believe it. That's something for them to decide within their perception of what's best for them.

And another thing: a "best product" cannot exist even if you think you've honestly found it. The word *best* is subjective. It's nothing more than an opinion. Those who don't recognize this cannot correctly communicate with prospects. They'll almost always fail and never know why. It's nearly a guaranteed outcome.

Now, let's read the first two paragraphs again. Perceptions, not products, are what you're "selling." And your prospect's perceptions of your product or service are what your prospects are "buying."

You may never have thought of the world this way. That's okay because until you fully grasp the power of perceptions it's difficult to know this. Ponder this for a while. Experiment with yourself and your ideas about the world and the things in it. Talk to your friends about it. You'll probably hear their opinions. But remember: an opinion only derives from their own perception of their world. Their own reality.

Certainly, you can find all kinds of things that you can identify as real, and they are real. Buildings are real. Trees are real. Highways are real. We can go on and on about what's real. But the point of understanding perceptions is in the difference in the way one perceives these real things compared to the way others perceive these real things. Differing perceptions of the same thing are actually quite common.

To one who is passionate about architecture, some buildings are breathtakingly beautiful. Seeing a building designed by Frank Lloyd Wright, I. M. Pei, Mies van der Rohe, Le Corbusier, or other great architects can take one's breath away. Well, you get the idea, so I won't go into a civil engineer's perception of the beauty of a great highway exchange, or an arborist's perception of the beauty of a tree, although Joyce Kilmer did write a nice poem about the beauty of a tree.

Yet many people don't see these things. They pass by buildings and streets that are so ugly they make your eyes hurt and cause severe headaches. They can offend one's sensibilities. They're a blight on the cityscape, yet many people aren't conscious of even seeing them, the ugliness, the blight. It's their perception of normal, so it doesn't even cross their minds.

This applies to everything in the world. People only see or hear in the frame of reference of their world view, that is to say, their perceptions. If you believe others perceive the same reality of the world that you do, then your marketing and advertising will be devastated by your error.

To help you discover for yourself why this is true, let's examine one instance of this. Visualize the following in your mind's eye so you'll feel it instead of just reading it.

You and a friend enjoy going to flea markets. Visualize this. You're standing in a flea market. You've just walked in, and you both happen to see a chair setting right in the front of the store.

Now a chair is a common thing. Everyone knows what a chair is. But knowing what a chair is, and feeling what a particular chair is, brings us to perceptions. Perceptions exist about everything we see or hear in the world. Even a chair.

Let's say that you happen to be into antique furniture, so you see it's a Duncan Phyfe chair. Wow! You know that presently there is a genuine Duncan Phyfe chair for sale on the internet for several thousand dollars. (This is true as I write this.)

Yet your friend who cares not a whit about antique furniture sees nothing but an old chair like he sat on for dinner at his grandmother's every Sunday for years.

You're both seeing the same chair, yet you both understand it differently. Completely differently. That's two different perceptions of the same thing. If we agree that perception is reality, then this is more than only that. It's two different realities about the same thing.

Perception is your mind's way of organizing things to make sense of the world for you personally. In this comparison, your mind sees an antique, a very interesting thing in your mind. Your friend sees an old chair. Also, familiar, but wholly uninteresting in your friend's mind.

If you tried to convince your friend that the old chair is very valuable, your friend will shrug his shoulders. He simply doesn't care about an old chair no matter what it is because your friend came to the flea market to find Elvis memorabilia. But you have so little interest in Elvis memorabilia that it's not even in your top thousand things of interest.

Yet it's what he values. It's what he wants personally. And he really can't believe you don't care about it. You'll never understand collecting Elvis stuff. And your friend will never understand why you like antique furniture. And that's the rub. Perceptions.

There's an old hackneyed expression: "Beauty is in the eyes of the beholder." Perceptions again. They've been known about for long, long time.

Through the processes of commonsense thinking and research, your marketing effort will reveal perceptions of your product generally held by your prospects and customers.

At first, you might think that if your prospect's perceptions of your product are different than your perceptions of your product, well then, the prospect just doesn't understand. They don't get it.

I promise you this will happen until you settle into understanding that each person sees and experiences things as being real through their own lens, their own perceptions. Reality is only what people perceive it to be. It differs in many ways; subtle, emotional ways.

By the way, animals also have perceptions. Your dog might hate kids and won't go near them because in the past he knows they've pulled his ears. My cat hates my wife's cat. Jealousy, I suspect. An old cat we have hates everything and everyone. But I digress. We aren't selling to animals, although it would be easy since dogs will believe anything.

Differing perceptions of reality are a good thing. What would the world be like if everything people saw, smelled, touched, heard, or tasted was exactly the same to them? If we perceived everything exactly the same way? We'd have nothing to talk about or discuss. It would be boring. Most likely, life would be so uninteresting and indescribably boring we'd have gone extinct a long time ago in blithering fits of madness.

But don't worry. It can't happen. Each individual's mind is far too complex for that; far more complex than we can understand.

PERCEPTION IS REALITY

REALITY LEAVES A LOT TO THE IMAGINATION.
—John Lennon

Each person relies on his or her perceptions to identify what's real. You'll come to realize that the perceptions held by customers and prospects are the only reality that matters.

People live, think, and exist in their own reality. So naturally, their perceptions are the only truth there is for them. And it does leave a lot to their imaginations and to yours. Work with their imaginations.

If you look deeply enough into how and why your customers and prospects perceive your products as they do, with an understanding of the emotional framework of their perceptions, you'll know how to engage them personally. And you'll find the keys to your marketing, advertising, and sales.

Remember that all advertising and communication with your target prospect and customer is personal. And there's a reason for that. All communications must be perceived to be personal or the message falls on deaf ears. Ask yourself: Who's going to listen to a message meant for someone else? Not many.

This is always true and unwavering. It's one of the organic marketplace's natural laws.

The upshot of this is that you can accomplish very little unless and until you understand your market well enough to think like your prospects and customers think. Said in a different way, their perceptions are their reality, and you must communicate with them within their reality, which is to say, within their perceptions. Nothing else matters.

There are no shortcuts to this. It's always about understanding your customers well enough to address their needs, wants and problems, personally. That always means "within their perceptions."

This new marketplace we're working in is about relationships. Not transactions. In this new, busier, and fast-paced marketplace, we must strive for engagement. And engagement requires more than understanding the consumers' perceptions. Engagement means understanding them emotionally and doing so with empathy.

Empathy is the beginning of all relationships. Relationships grow only when you can truly empathize with the consumer. This is when you can reach the point of engagement with your customer.

Engagement means your prospects and customers have come to trust you and your company, and that's primarily because of the way you communicate with them.

So, you must nurture the relationship by listening to and understanding the perceptions of your prospects and customers. Over time, this will cause the relationship to grow deeper.

Never misunderstand that engagement with your prospects and customers is a process that requires a highly developed emotional intelligence, that is, knowing their emotional needs through empathy and insight and exhibiting a regard for their needs.

Your emotional intelligence is a golden tool. Don't ignore it. Many experts believe your emotional intelligence, your EQ, is just as important to your success as your intelligence quotient, your IQ. Maybe more.

I would say probably more.

EMOTIONAL INTELLIGENCE IS AS POWERFUL AS INTELLECTUAL INTELLIGENCE

VALUING CUSTOMERS' AND PROSPECTS' PERCEPTIONS WITH EMPATHY IS THE KEY TO SUCCESSFUL ENGAGEMENT.

As a marketer, you must strive to create relationships with your customers because relationships are lasting. Transactions aren't.

All relationships begin with the customers' perception of an expectation of trust. That makes their perceptions the most important thing in your marketing effort.

Understanding your prospects' and customers' perceptions means you understand them as people. A personal perception goes far in building trust. Remember that all advertising is personal. People can feel that. They respond to it. It creates trust and loyalty. Yet trust isn't automatically given. Trust must be earned and demonstrated continually by staying in touch with your prospects and customers. Probably for a lot longer time and with more personal contacts than you think.

There's a reason for this. Not all your prospects are ready to buy your product the first time you contact them. Some are, but most aren't. However, a qualified prospect will most likely buy from you at some point in time, but their need and time is later. If you remain in touch with them, empathetically and personally, you'll be there when they make the decision to buy.

Ask yourself how often you've liked a product, but you've put off buying it for one reason or another. Maybe you're traveling, or maybe you don't want to pay for it right now, or maybe you know you won't use it now, but you likely will in six months. There are a variety of reasons. In no way does this mean you aren't interested. Only poor salespeople would assume this. Very poor salespeople.

Businesses need to train their salespeople to achieve the best results. They're the last and final contact point between your business and a new customer. If they drop the ball and fail to engage a prospect, then you're wasting more than just their salaries. You're also wasting your advertising dollars.

This brings me to briefly discuss sales. It's astonishing that three (3) is the average number of times salespeople make contacts, then quit because they assume there's no interest by the prospect. What!! After all the time and money spent to attract a prospect, the average salesperson gives up after three contacts. You can be sure that it took more than three times seeing your advertising for a person to become a prospect. Studies on exposure of your advertising show that it takes seven to ten exposures to your targeted audience/market to create a sales lead.

That requires a substantial investment. The average salesperson needs a kick start.

Microsoft says it contacts prospects from ten to twenty times. Think about it. After the tenth time, Microsoft is probably the only company still contacting the prospect. So, would you say there's nearly a 100 percent likelihood that the prospect will buy from Microsoft when the time is right for them? It certainly increases the odds, doesn't it?

As a business owner or manager, you must teach your salespeople how the product is perceived by prospects and customers. Even about how the salespeople themselves are perceived by prospects and customers.

Show them why some products require specific approaches, presentations, demonstrations, and engagement to sell. Good salespeople should already know this instinctively. Mediocre-to-poor salespeople don't.

It's part of having emotional intelligence. Your emotional intelligence tells you it's best for your business to remain in contact with your prospects, even though they haven't purchased a thing so far.

It doesn't matter how smart you are. Success doesn't come from having great intelligence (not that it doesn't help). In the long-term, success comes from having good emotional intelligence; a personal involvement with your customers and prospects and their needs, because that's what relationships are built on. And that creates engagement with trust.

The following short illustration is about how relationships are formed on a personal level by a good salesperson.

A man goes to a hardware store to buy a power drill. But he doesn't really need a drill. You, as an astute salesperson, instinctively know that all he needs are holes.

Selling is a process. So, here's how emotional intelligence makes a big difference. Your prospect has an emotional need for holes, which means he has an emotional investment in the reason he needs holes.

As we know, emotions drive every personal contact and every decision. Every contact, transaction, or exchange is deeper than most people think because everything stems from emotions. Everything. And this is completely overlooked most of the time.

You know this customer needs holes. There aren't many other reasons for a drill.

So, you're offered an opportunity to help a customer satisfy his need emotionally and do so personally. First, you make sure the drill you show him will solve his problem and give him the exact holes he needs. But . . .

Let's say the customer only thinks he needs holes, so using your emotional intelligence, you listen closely to his questions. And you learn that he needs to insert rods into these holes.

Considering what he needs, you realize that fasteners would work better than holes. And you explain why this would be the best solution to his need. He's delighted with your suggestion, and he feels you've really been helpful. And you sell him some fasteners.

There, you've truly solved the customer's problem, and you've solved it personally on an emotional level. Solving problems—fulfilling needs is what a business does. The best businesses do it on an emotional level.

Now you should also notice that you've also created trust. You've created a customer who feels you're sort of like a helpful friend. It's an emotional thing. After this, you're someone he feels he can come to for help with his next need or problem. And he'll come back to you again and again because he trusts you to help him solve problems and fulfill his needs. That's engagement. And you can see how powerful it is.

The next time you go into a store to see about buying a drill, or anything else, and the salesperson yells to you, "They're over on aisle five," you'll feel the difference, emotionally. You'll feel as though you're nothing more than another warm body in the store. And that's all you are in that store. Eventually, you'll stop going to that store.

Let's look at some major study findings from of a lengthy report on studies and analysis of emotional engagement published by Alan Zorfas and Daniel Leemon in the *Harvard Business Review.*

Their study findings show us that on a lifetime value basis, "emotionally connected customers" are more than twice as valuable as what we might call "highly satisfied customers." Their study tells us that emotionally connected customers buy more of your products and services, visit you more often, exhibit less price sensitivity, pay more attention to your communications, follow your advice, and recommend you more to others.

Emotional connections and engagement suddenly mean a lot more to you, don't they? Everything is about emotions, perceptions and engagement. Everything.

Etch this into your mind. These are the most important and consequential aspects of getting and keeping customers and very few marketers understand them. But the best marketers do.

Yet few people even realize there are emotional connections. Even fewer know that emotions have anything to do with buying. They resist the idea. They're certain that all their buying decisions are derived from their intellect. Once you deeply understand perceptions and emotions, this idea would make a cat laugh.

And there's more. People with high EI are usually successful in most things they do. Why? Because they're people who others relate to easier, because they're emotionally astute. They're what we refer to as *people people.* This is a valuable quality, an imperative, to establish in your marketing and a vital ability in your salespeople.

In his book titled *Emotional Intelligence—Why It Can Matter More Than IQ,*[4] Daniel Goleman, an American psychologist, developed a framework of five elements that define emotional intelligence:

1. **Self-Awareness**—People with high EI are usually very self-aware. They understand their emotions, and because of this, they're confident. They trust their intuition. People who study this believe that self-awareness is the most important part of emotional intelligence.

---

[4] © 1995, Daniel Goleman

2. **Self-Regulation**—This is the ability to control emotions and impulses. High EI people don't make impulsive, careless decisions.

3. **Motivation**—People with a high degree of EI are usually motivated. They're willing to defer immediate results for long-term success; delayed gratification. They're highly productive and love a challenge, and so they're very effective in whatever they do.

4. **Empathy**—This is perhaps the second most-important element of EI. Empathy is the ability to identify with and understand the wants, needs, and viewpoints of others. People with empathy are good at recognizing the feelings of others, even when those feelings may not be obvious. We've all heard the saying "don't judge a person until you've walked a mile in their shoes". That's empathy explained differently. They avoid stereotyping and judging too quickly. As a result, empathetic people are usually excellent at relationships, listening, and relating to others.

5. **Social Skills**—It's unusually easy to talk to and to like people with good social skills, which are another sign of high EI. Those with strong social skills typically help others with their needs. They're excellent communicators and are masters at building and maintaining relationships. They have the attributes for being leaders.

The best salespeople have a high emotional intelligence. Recall the floor salesperson who helped the man who thought he needed a drill. His EI enabled him to satisfy the customer on an emotional level of engagement that's crucial to keeping customers.

Emotional intelligence has not been fully recognized or discussed at length since it was first quantified in the mid-1990s. So very few people, including marketers, know its depth and significance.

Although intellectual intelligence is important to success in life, many people believe emotional intelligence is at least as important. Now that EI is more fully understood and recognized, many companies use EI testing in hiring.

EI is the capacity to value others, listen to their wants and needs, and empathize, or identify, with them on different levels. Emotional intelligence is how engagement happens in your marketing and communications efforts. This is a major element in rethinking marketing in the new marketplace.

As we move through this book, we'll discover more about perceptions; how to define your marketplace and then how to understand it. And then, the more well-defined your marketplace becomes.

A LACK OF EMOTIONAL INTELLIGENCE PUT A WHOLE COMPANY AT RISK

COMMUNICATION DIDN'T SEEM IMPORTANT.

We were asked by a jet aircraft defense contractor to help them determine why their employees seemed to be unhappy and seemed to feel alienated. Management was seriously concerned they would lose valuable employees.

Using a simple inquiry-interview method I call an "internal audit," we set out to learn about the problem and what might be done about it by interviewing up to thirty people randomly throughout the company, including management and the employees who worked in the factory.

The problem was clear from the first few interviews. But the thing of it was, the management had no clue because they had little, if any, emotional intelligence. And except for the plant managers, they had almost no contact with the employees.

This company was seriously old-school, top-down, heavy-handed management. Since they did business only as a government contractor, they had adapted the government's way of doing things. Few things can be as mind-numbingly ponderous and impersonal as government systems.

The employees in fabrication and assembly, even those working on the line, felt they didn't know what was going on. They said they were only told what to do and given deadlines for it, but they were told nothing about anything else. They felt ignored. Not respected for their work. These are vital personal emotions and perceptions.

After explaining the findings of our internal audit to management, we got their undivided attention. They had no idea. (But, how could they? They never talked to their people.) We proposed a project to keep everyone informed and engaged personally and emotionally.

For this, our solution was to develop a weekly newsletter that went to everyone in the company. The first requirement was that it had to be the same newsletter with the same content for everyone, including everyone in management. Management was intrigued by the idea but didn't think they had to be a part of it. But, yes, they did. Their lack of involvement is what had caused the problem we were solving. They were not managers. They were rulers.

This newsletter had to be much different than the typical external newsletter used for attracting customers. Those are generally filled with product information, new products, improvements on the features of their product, and maybe showing a new wing being built on the factory, and so on. To say these are not stimulating to the employees is an understatement.

So, it couldn't be written with any empathy by management. That was a given. It could only be written by us because we could be objective and empathetic about the perceptions of the people, both employees and management. We understood the need for personal and emotional content. And we knew how to do it. Recognizing and using the perceptions of the employees was, of course, the key, and that made it a success.

One of our staff writers had been a newspaper reporter, so she was an excellent interviewer and took accurate notes. This was a fun assignment for her. She would go to the factory every week for interviews, the latest news of the company, the employees and management, and return to write the newsletter in two days on a deadline, so we got the newsletter to the company while the news was still fresh.

We maintained control of the process, the most important thing of all, since management didn't realize that anyone even had perceptions. They didn't understand the concept. But our compelling case for it, the internal audit, enabled us to go ahead with it.

That everyone received the same newsletter made it work very well. It informed everyone of new contracts being negotiated in Washington, much to the relief of the people working on the factory floor that they would continue to have jobs.

We even informed everyone when an employee or their family, whether management or factory personnel, had a birthday or a baby, or celebrated a wedding anniversary. Wishing each person at the company a happy birthday on the week of their birthday was extremely popular. Photos were taken. People in the pictures were smiling. Everyone felt a new positive attitude in the company.

It was a good feeling to know we had succeeded. The employees perceived themselves to be part of the group, and now everyone knew how everyone contributed to the company. I wouldn't go so far as to say they became like a family. But they were happy and satisfied because they knew what was going on, and they felt it on a personal, emotional level.

Management was happy that their problem had been solved with such an all-inclusive solution good for the employees and good for the company. The last I heard from them; they were still publishing their newsletter.

On a related subject, it may surprise you to learn that many companies don't know what business they're in. It's not as uncommon as one might think among many businesses big and small, and in fact, among whole industries. The next chapter might surprise you. And alert you.

NOT UNDERSTANDING THE BUSINESS ONE IS IN CAN CAUSE COMPANIES AND EVEN WHOLE INDUSTRIES TO FAIL

SOME CAN'T SEE THE FOREST BECAUSE A BUNCH OF TREES ARE BLOCKING THE VIEW.

This is a cautionary tale as you set out in your business. It's an anecdote for you about a business that didn't understand its purpose. But worse, they misunderstood what business they were in. A business can fail, and management honestly won't know why. Here's a real-life example of how it can happen.

Several years ago, I had a client in the wire-manufacturing business, a large company in business for nearly a century. They made all kinds of wire: steel, cooper, silver, aluminum, and so on. And they did it well.

Because of the high quality of their products, most all their sales were to those needing quality materials, such as electronics companies that manufactured telephones, radios, TVs, computers, and such. The manufacturer had great quality control and a great product, yet they had a problem they shouldn't have had and didn't know why.

We'd been referred to them by another client to help them with their marketing and advertising. Later, they became a client, but as you'll see, that wasn't a result I would've bet on.

In our initial meeting, the CEO and the sales manager said sales were slipping and they couldn't figure out why. They were very worried. They were a long-established company with a good reputation for their products and their business methods. So why were they not doing better each year instead of continually selling less?

It's always good to learn as much as possible about a company before meeting with a group of the company's decision-makers, in this case the board of directors. And I had done my homework. Again, experience is helpful, so I thought I knew the problem after our first meeting. This happens a lot. First impressions and first remarks can be very telling if one is listening closely and at least partially understands the situation.

It seemed they were so close to the old-line industry of wire making that they couldn't see beyond it. You know the old saw about being too close the trees to see the forest. So, I simply asked the board what business they were in. Well, that created a stir.

The managers and directors in the meeting looked at me as if to say, "OMG, we're wasting our time with a dunce." They perceived me to be asking what they manufactured, but that wasn't my question. That was my fault. No matter what, we're always dealing with the perceptions of others. And I hadn't articulated my question well enough.

I laughed when I saw their expressions. Well, what else was I to do? I quickly recovered while the thought was still hanging in the air and restated it by asking them what industry segment they served. And what businesses are their customers and end users in?

But the ominous looks in their eyes told me they still didn't get what I was prodding them for. You see, I wanted them to come up with the answer themselves. A problem well stated is half solved.

Sometimes one can be too subtle. But if they could answer the question themselves, they could immediately internalize it.

I explained that from what I knew about their company so far, it appeared that they were in the communication business. I went on to push them further by reminding them that their largest, most important, and probably, most profitable customers/end users were in the communication business in one form or another. So that essentially meant they were in the communications business too, since their sales records revealed that they almost totally served that industry.

I'll never forget that moment. They looked totally dumbstruck. I thought, *Oh crap, they still don't get it. I'll be thrown out the door like a javelin.*

Then it was as if a light dawned on each of them. Well, anyway, they all had strange, eyebrow-raising expressions.

The CEO, sitting at the head of the conference table, looked at me and shook his head. Oh crap, again. He was going to give me his thought in two words: "Get out, you idiot." Okay, four words.

But in fact, he said, "I doubt that has ever occurred to any of us, but you're absolutely right." I stood there for a moment to make sure I heard him right, and I saw him smiling.

Sigh of relief.

Strangely, I was then considered to be a by-god genius, a veritable wizard. Not a dunce after all.

As an aside: it's humbling to come home after a day of being a genius, only to be assured by my wife that it's only my perception.

Some very smart people in businesses and even whole industries have succeeded only to fail later, because they became so familiar with the business that they couldn't see the forest for the trees. Familiarity, as I wrote earlier, can cause anyone to overlook the obvious.

This wasn't the only time I came across this phenomenon. It happens more frequently than one would think. One reason is that many of the people in management are out of touch with their customers.

So, I learned that one of the first things to do upon acquiring a new client was the internal audit that I mentioned earlier, to learn what the people throughout the company thought about their jobs, about what the company was, and what business they thought the company was in.

To dissuade management that I wasn't being condescending, or being presumptuous, I assured them this was not an uncommon problem. In fact, I explained, it was so common that I had developed a method of determining it. Its resulting analysis and its execution assures that everyone in the company is on the same page. And it's also the first step of developing a marketing plan. They warmed to that quickly.

Management is responsible to the owner or to the shareholders for making the business profitable. There is no other reason for a business to exist. That's so obvious it's hardly worth saying. (Even not-for-profit businesses need to succeed and be profitable although the means and ends differ.)

Management is generally the first to get into a rut and stop thinking about these kinds of things. It's the duty and nature of management to pursue goals, not to philosophize, which is how they usually regard this.

In doing our internal audit, I insisted on interviewing each person separately so one person's ideas didn't taint another person's ideas. (Which, by the way, is a big problem in finding the true attitudes of people in a focus group, and why I don't recommend them. More about that later.)

A simple list of questions to learn about how each person in management and elsewhere in the company perceives the business of the company reveals what is otherwise not known or ignored.

As I explained, following the internal audit, I return to management with a report of my findings. Usually a short report of a few pages can cover the findings.

You'll probably find something of this nature to be helpful to you in your own business, even about your own ideas.

It helps to improve and focus your own objectivity and to assure that you and your own people are all on the same page. Be cautious. Objectivity is a slippery will-o'-the-wisp to grasp and hold.

It's a reminder of the power of the organic marketplace. Not paying attention to it can be brutal. And it takes no prisoners.

THE CONSUMER IS NOT A MORON

SHE IS YOUR WIFE.

-David Ogilvy
From *Ogilvy on Advertising*

To underestimate your prospect or customer simply because we think they hold the wrong perceptions (How could anyone think like that, for god's sake?) is a mental trap full of unintended consequences.

When you consciously, or unconsciously, underestimate your prospects or customers, they can feel it in the message you're sending them. Frankly, you're being condescending. Even arrogant. That's not a message you would send if you wish to get and keep new customers. Yet such an attitude comes through quite readily in any message, advertisement, or email. I've seen these kinds of expressions in advertisements and emails solicitations and so have you. They're repellent.

You see, others have had different experiences than you or me. Their experiences have contributed to their perceptions, even created their perceptions. They've seen the world differently through the lenses of their lives. Their perceptions are different, but they're just as valid as mine or yours.

How smart you are, or how smart your prospect is, has nothing to do with perceptions, or their propensity to react to your message and to buy your product or service. Whether one agrees or not doesn't really matter. Only perceptions matter. It's the way the mind works.

Perceptions, as do emotions, originate in what is loosely referred to as the right brain. That is, the right brain processes thoughts in visuals and symbols and in strict terms. There are no gray areas. They're rigid and unshakable, so much so that some psychologists refer to "right brain equations" because they're fixed in the mind like an equation. To the right brain, a thing is either right or wrong, good or bad, up or down, black or white. But it's spot-on correct in each person's mental vocabulary. It's somewhat primal since it evolved from the necessity of our ancestors to stay alive. Its reactions are quick and intuitive, instinctive.

It makes sense then that our long-term memory resides in the right brain (along with our primordial survival instincts nearby in the hypothalamus, the reptilian brain, that controls our autonomic system).

The evidence shows we have visual memories. Dreams originate in the right brain. Our memories do not come to our minds in words. They come to mind as pictures, visualizations of what is recalled. When someone says red, the mind visualizes the color, not the word.

Read any good books lately? Why were they good? Because you visualized them.

Dr. Carl Sagan wrote in his book *The Dragons of Eden* that our primordial memories remain vitally in touch with our conscious minds. One example he used was that elevators universally use a green light to indicate the elevator is going up but uses a red light to indicate it's going down. Our minds are hardwired for color. Red is a color associated with danger in most all cultures, and a red light on the elevator warns us we are going down, derived from the fear of falling (out of our tree), the most ancient of all fears in our minds. Quaintly stated, there are predators and probable death waiting down there. Red is also used in traffic lights to mean to stop, or chance being injured. A red flag is a warning that something's not right. Fascinating, isn't it? Red is also the color of blood, a thing most people can't tolerate, especially if it's our own.

The right brain's processes are defined by perceptions since the right brain thinks only in visuals; symbols and pictures. Some experts believe that the right brain remembers everything one has ever seen (stored as a visual memory). To have a photographic memory simply means to have perfect recall from the right brain.

Have you ever noticed that people who can remember long tracts or entire books and are asked to recall them almost always close their eyes? And if you watch closely, you can see eye movements under their eyelids moving from left to right and back as if they're visualizing the page(s) and reading from a visual memory. It seems they're doing just this.

As an aside, many autistics and savants have incredible right brain abilities, particularly with memory. Look up the study about an autistic person who was taken on one flight over Rome and, from seeing the city once, was able to draw an accurate and very detailed map of the city. Nearly unbelievable, but true. This is extremely interesting to me.

The so-called left brain (the cerebral cortex) contains reading, speech, language, and abilities for mathematical calculations and many other higher cognitive abilities. But along with that, the left brain has the uncanny ability to rationalize anything. It's a very flexible and adaptable ability of "reasoning" that allows anything to be filed under "reasons why."

Both hemispheres, right and left brain, have many connections to each other. They're in constant communication. That means there's a constant subconscious struggle going on between both. The right brain sees only absolutes, and the left brain/cerebellum makes of it whatever it wants.

This accounts for the conflicts we have in our minds. Some conflicts are small, like what I want for dinner as opposed to what I'm really going to have because I forgot to buy potatoes. But then some are so great, so intense, that they create terrifying conflicts in the right brain.

An unwanted and irreconcilable upheaval or change in a person's life can be stressful. But if it goes too far with an impossibly irreconcilable difference, it's perceived by the right brain as death of the (psychological) self.

Psychological death of self means that who you perceive yourself to be as a person no longer exists because of the change to "who you have become." This is perceived by the right brain as being no different than actual physical death.

Divorce, going to prison, death of a loved one, having an unwanted pregnancy, or losing a job can cause horrifying conflicting emotions that are perceived as being no different than death.

Don't get all wacked-out about this. Remember: the things about a left brain/right brain struggle I've described must be considered unwanted, or very undesirable, or they wouldn't create a conflict.

If a person has made their career the total definition of who they are, then losing their job is perceived to be that they're no longer that person. To the right brain, they no longer have a life. This is the same as if they had died; the psychological equivalent of death.

Many women could not be happier to become pregnant. They would love to be mothers. But to an eighteen-year-old woman who plans to go to college, or an unmarried woman who's just arriving in her career, pregnancy may seem to be the end of her world. In the left brain/right brain struggle, she would become something she doesn't want to be. A mother. And the right brain perceives that as the "death of self." They're no longer the person they were, and they experience the most devastating of all emotions; a complete loss of faith and hope for the future. The need and ability to look to the future with faith and hopefulness is a psychological imperative for us humans.

Airsickness is caused by a life-or-death conflict between the right brain and the left. The left brain with cognitive abilities can comprehend remaining stationary in a seat while traveling hundreds of miles per hour in the air, which is invisible. However, the right brain cannot grasp this, and a struggle ensues between cognition and the nonverbal visuals of the right brain. The struggle becomes so intense that finally the right brain is convinced the body has been poisoned. So, it vomits the perceived poison. And that's the need for the handy bags on the back of the passenger's seats.

Although there's a lot more to this, at least this provides some understanding of how the mind deals with perceptions. And it's not so clean and linear as some might believe. It's complicated. It must not be treated lightly. It's a deep thing, very deep, and it has near absolute staying power.

So, in consumer marketing studies, we can't simply ask someone what they think about a thing because we'll only hear what they think they think. They're sincere, but they're only able to tell you how their left brain has rationalized a thing to be.

Rationalizations are the little subconscious lies we tell ourselves to justify our actions. The left brain can rationalize anything to keep the human being in sync with all the other rationalizations it has filed away.

Understand that the left brain lies a lot. Be careful of it.

History, along with conventional thinking, can mislead us into believing we know something that we don't know.

Ralph Waldo Emerson once advised, "Build a better mousetrap and the world will beat a path to your door." These were words of encouragement for the American spirit of innovation and entrepreneurship. And Emerson's quote has been the byword for new inventions, new products, and new innovations for years.

But comes a major shift in the business paradigm, and it's no longer true. Such as now. Currently, the marketplace is moving at an ever-increasing speed, and consumers no longer act and react to the marketplace as they did in the past.

About Ralph's claim, "the world will beat a path to your door," well, I'm not going to kid you. You'll have to work very hard to get a path going.

A better product is not enough. A better product does not guarantee any level of success. And in the larger faster high-tech world we live in, no one will beat a path to your door. They won't even know you have a door.

But your prospects and customers can and will find your door if you understand marketing and how marketing enables effective advertising; the ability to communicate with your prospects and customers within their perceptions.

And that in turn, enables changes in their perceptions. So, in effect, you can show them where your door is. Done well, they'll know which door they're looking for. Great marketers build roads to their doors.

RUN FROM CONVENTIONAL THINKING

IT WILL ONLY GIVE YOU CONVENTIONAL IDEAS, AND THAT'S NOT GOOD ENOUGH.

Here's a springboard to new ideas and new ways of thinking. Once you get into it and get the hang of thinking this way, you'll come up with new thoughts, insights, and probably some really crazy stuff.

Crazy stuff is a good thing. Scare yourself with new ideas. Don't discount anything as being too wild or off the wall. Instead, write them down, all of them. Even the crazy stuff. Let them cool off for a while. Then come back to them, explore them, consider them from all angles.

Nine out of ten times, one of these will be the spark that sets you on a course to discovery. You can stretch it, massage it, pull it, push it, rewrite it, and you have a start.

A start is all you need at this point.

Now relax and give yourself permission to free your mind from "the terms in which we have been conducted to think," and I promise you can reach your prospects and customers in the most effective way possible. It's magical. (That's just a metaphor. There's no such thing as magic.)

Yet it really can be a magical process, fascinating and exciting too. But it's absolutely necessary for success.

So, let me say it again. Stretch your mind. Push through the ordinary. Think from the inside out, then think again from the outside in. Constantly remind yourself that conventional thinking will only give you conventional ideas. And those are not good enough.

Dance on the edge. Look up over the side of the trench you're in. See the horizon. That is where you should be headed.

David Ogilvy, in my opinion, a genius in advertising, once said, and I paraphrase a bit, "Don't swing the bat just to hit the ball. Swing as hard as you can. Try to knock it out of the ballpark. After all, that's what you ought to be aiming for."

THE GREATEST MYTH

THE TRUTH WILL BE APPARENT, SO THE BEST PRODUCT WINS.

Those who are unknowingly relying on luck, and don't know what they don't know, can have their customers taken from them anytime another marketer offers them a better deal. More businesses fit this description than you might imagine.

People believe what they want to believe. And many, if not most, think the truth will always be apparent, so ultimately the best product wins. Naturally, they think their product is the best. Naturally, customers will swoop in and buy it.

This is the greatest myth in business and marketing. It's self-delusion by those who aren't willing to make the effort to understand their products, their marketplaces, or their customers. It destroys fledgling businesses before they get off the ground. These marketers believe that the truth will always be apparent. At least, their version of the truth. That's the delusion.

"Truth" has been pursued since the beginning of time. It's one of philosophy's oldest questions. Can you honestly say you know the truth about anything? I say there is no such thing as the "truth," or the "best product." They're both perceptions.

Said another way: There is no objective reality, no objective truth. There's only perception. But here's the thing. Perceptions are realities, so how do we define the perception of truth?

Well, we don't. And here's why. It doesn't matter.

If there's an objective truth, how would we know? Who would tell us? Another person looking at the same thing. That's nothing more than another person's perception. So, we look for an expert opinion. And who's an expert? It's someone who's perceived to be an expert in the mind of someone else. A perception again.

Emotions are strong things. They dominate our reality and our reactions to our reality. So, they dominate our perceptions. It may stun you to realize that many people make buying decisions based on secondhand perceptions; someone else's perception of reality. How weird is that? Yet it happens all the time.

I even have a name for this. I call it the "everyone knows principle". Clever, eh. Here's how it works in one instance:

"Everyone knows" Japanese cars are better than American cars.

"Everyone knows" if you have a bad experience with a Japanese car, you were just unlucky. "Everyone knows" if you have a bad experience with an American made car, well, "everyone knows" American cars aren't as good as Japanese cars.

Do you believe that? Is it true? It doesn't matter. People think what they want to think. We're in the marketplace and perceptions, not products, are the forces we reckon with every day.

What constitutes a product and what constitutes the perception of a product? This is a salient point. They're different. Ultimately, emotions govern everything we do. Every idea and attitude we hold, every decision we make, is emotionally driven.

Don't believe this? Well, many people who are highly educated and perceive themselves to be totally intellectually driven don't believe this either. They can't. Their self-image won't allow it. And yet, their self-image is derived from their emotional idea of who they are. Don't you love irony?

But do you believe it? If you don't, then I challenge you to identify any decision that's not based on an emotion, or several emotions. In fact, I'll go one further. I double-dog dare you to show me any act or decision that's not based on emotions. That's a dare no one can walk away from. Go ahead. Try to think of one such decision.

Let's start here with the intellectual chore of doing the proper accounting in operating a business. It's an emotionally driven action. The emotion driving us to do proper accounting is fear. Would you have guessed that?

We all do accounting because of fear: fear of not knowing if you're losing money; fear that your pricing is not covering costs; fear you may be losing customers because some items are priced too high. And then there's the really big fear of the IRS, and the need of having accurate tax returns backed up with documentation.

You might substitute the word *fear* and use the word *concern*. But regardless of the synonym used to describe it, the emotion is fear.

Another way of realizing that emotions drive everything is to look at medical doctors. Doctors are very intelligent and highly educated. Yet they're wholly driven by emotion all the while making learned intellectual decisions about diagnosis, medication, treatments, and so on.

Think not? Then consider this. Why would they go through all the rigors of a university education in a very difficult curriculum and then spend another four to six years in medical school, and two to four more years if they're specializing? And then subject themselves to the intensity of two years or more of internship and residency?

All this so they can work fifteen hours a day, seeing patients one after another all day long, and then be called to the hospital in the middle of the night, or the middle of a symphony concert, or while dining with friends?

Here's why. They have an emotional need to care for people. This is a very strong emotional need. It's found in all caregivers. Doctors are extremely emotionally driven. But Medicine being such a scientific and fact-driven pursuit, most people would think it was a purely intellectual, clinical objectivity.

Good doctors know it's not.

STUDIES IN MARKETING INCOMPETENCE

WHO ARE YOU GOING TO BELIEVE?
ME, OR YOUR LYING EYES?

—Groucho Marx

Some companies honestly think that their products or services are somehow different, that it's so well-known and accepted that the rules don't apply to them. Yet they almost always fail. So why does this thinking persist?

General Motors is an example of this thinking. I know this because I've had experience working with this company and saw the end coming long before GM went broke in 2007.

I continue wondering why. If I could see it, why couldn't they?

Too much ego involved. They believed their own propaganda. Self-delusion. Sycophants in the executive suites. Lots of lame excuses, but no real reasons.

Remember earlier, when I said that every business in any marketplace is subject to the same natural laws and the same rules? They're always present and never vary. This is big. I know I've mentioned this several times, but never let it slip to second place in your mind.

You must understand your marketplace. Those who don't will fail, and they'll never know why. GM's people didn't, or wouldn't, understand their marketplace, and in 2007 GM failed. Went flat broke. Bankrupt after a hundred years of doing the same job.

Every succeeding management group retained nothing in a century of operating a business. No institutional knowledge seemed to carry from one management group to the next.

When GM failed, they blamed their problems on their workers' wages and benefits, bad dealerships, hapless vendors, the economy, and so on to the limits of imagination. They blamed everything except the single most important thing: The consumers' perception of the value and quality of their vehicles.

GM never gave that a thought. It didn't matter to them. Seriously. It did not. Their attitude was, *We'll build 'em, and they'll buy 'em, just like we always have.* GM is a case study in arrogance and incompetence.

GM brass ignored the findings of consumer psychology studies about what people wanted in a car even though they paid for the studies to be done. They took the customer's loyalty to the GM brand for granted.

Oldsmobile, one their oldest and most well-known brands, was degraded to increase profits with no concern for customers who had religiously driven Oldsmobiles for years. Oldsmobile's Rocket 88 and 98 engines were legendary. Considered the best engines on the market. GM replaced them with Chevrolet engines. And proceeded to cheapen everything about the car, all the while advertising, "This isn't your father's Oldsmobile." Well, they got that right.

A consumer psychologist I worked with warned GM that each badge or model was a steppingstone to the next higher level. Removing Oldsmobile from the brand line-up would devastate Cadillac sales. GM refused to believe it. So, they did it, and it did.

The root cause of why they went broke is simple. They killed the process and the reasons for customer loyalty, the most valuable thing a brand possesses.

In its genius, GM removed two of the major "steppingstones" of their customers' brand-loyalty advancement: Pontiac and Oldsmobile. So, their loyal customers paused at these thresholds, looked around, and discovered many other makes of cars in the same price range. Competitors' cars. And away they went. GM lost them as customers then and for the future. They betrayed their loyal customers. Unforgivable.

GM blamed the dealers for stabbing them in the back. The mind reels. It's hard to comprehend such thinking and decision making.

And I won't even to go into the story of GM's Saturn cars whose owners loved the cars so much they gathered annually for an owners' picnic near the factory in Tennessee. Ever hear of such a thing with any other car? None that I know of. GM didn't care. They even moved Saturn's manufacturing back to Detroit.

In fact, GM quit making the bestselling Saturn cars altogether and sold the brand to Opel. Opel now makes and sells Saturn cars, and they're doing quite well. Strokes of genius.

How does a company take three popular, multigenerational brand leaders and smash them to smithereens without a second thought?

GM is a perfect example of an almost inconceivable lack of understanding of their own products, customers brand loyalty and perceptions, and absolutely no understanding of their marketplace.

GM went broke in 2007. But it was thought to be too big to allow it to fail. So, it was resurrected by the government (taxpayers' money) so it could fail again, because the same mentality still exists there.

And it will fail again. Hide and watch because currently GM is whining that it cannot sell enough cars. So, in its nearly legendary ability to mismanage, GM is now saying they'll have to begin leasing all their vehicles to consumers, because too few buyers can be found. Can you imagine that? Neither can I. If a market exists for leasing cars, then there is a market for selling cars too. An auto lease is simply a sale of a different kind.

We have discovered that the organic marketplace has the same natural laws that consistently restrict, or enable, in the same ways no matter what the product or service is, or who is selling it. Even a big business. Especially big business.

In my experiences with big businesses, I've seen some unbelievable examples of bad decision making because of the isolated groupthink of large companies. And we've all seen them make some of the most spectacular mistakes because of it. As I've illustrated, GM is almost an expert at making bad decisions.

These companies are so large that the momentum they have can overcome their mistakes. Most of the time. It takes a lot of dumb decisions to knock down a huge company, but it happens.

Remember such marketplace giants as Kodak, Polaroid, Compaq, Nintendo? All of them were market leaders. Some for generations. They're still around today, a shadow of their former selves. Has-beens struggling in the bottom of the market. What happened?

Kodak actually invented the digital camera but couldn't imagine it had a future. What? No film? Film was a huge profit center for Kodak, so I don't know if they really wanted a digital camera on the market.

Polaroid intended for its product to be as handy as a phone. Polaroid said this out loud to its intended market. But then phones became instant cameras. Well, of all things.

Compaq and Nintendo didn't understand the businesses they were in. Or their marketplaces.

Nintendo's CEO decided since they were a veritable icon in digital games and had the largest market share (close to 90 percent), that they should become a computer company.

Brilliant.

Have you ever heard of a Nintendo computer? Neither has anyone else. Presently, Nintendo has about 10 percent of a market they once dominated. Go figure.

The CEO was fired, yet the downward spiral continued. I'm betting that the stockholders thought he should have been drawn, quartered, shot, stabbed, and hung (figuratively speaking, of course.)

It's not too difficult to understand how and why such incredibly stupid decisions were made. By far, the greatest cause of bad decisions is what takes place in the executive suite among people who think they're smart only because they surround themselves with sycophants, yes-men, who would agree with the boss if he said the sky was green.

Perceptions are one of the absolute truths of business. GM and others have never learned that. They almost seem to have contrived not to know this. Incredible. Prospects' and customers' perceptions about your product or service define your product and your marketplace. Their perceptions are reality, the reality you and your business must deal with every day. And the reality was that Nintendo is not a computer.

This isn't familiar territory for most people. And it's totally alien to some mentioned above. They simply don't believe perceptions matter. But any marketer who fights perceptions, or disregards them, will always lose. If you aren't communicating within your prospects' and customers' perceptions, then you're simply talking to yourself.

Let me take this thought s bit farther. Consider this. If a business doesn't know how its customers and prospects perceive their product, then why in the world does such a business expect to sell anything at all?

The big businesses mentioned earlier make a good case for rethinking marketing. But we won't be concentrating on them. Their business models are entirely different than yours. Yes, there are a few big businesses that are excellent at what they do. Amazon is one, and there are others.

That excellence comes from an extraordinary marketing plan and an extraordinary business plan and management's total commitment to it and to their customers. This is such a rare thing in big business that it's nearly unrecognizable. And Amazon's huge success is a rare thing in big business because it's constantly changing its tactics to remain viable and to meet or exceed the demands of the marketplace.

Most big businesses are behemoths nearly incapable of movement, or change. Their business models are not in sync with today's faster-paced marketplace because they cannot move quickly enough to address it. Any ill wind can take them out.

More publicly owned companies have gone broke last year than in any year in history. And more well-known public companies are set to fold this year.

The things we've discussed here are the biggest reason why. These companies don't understand their customers' perceptions, motivations, and barriers anymore (if they ever did), they're product oriented, not consumer oriented, and they're so large and top heavy they can't move quickly enough to regain their past positions in the marketplace or create a new position.

As a small business, you have the advantage. You can be flexible, unrestricted, and ignore "the way it's always been done." You can move faster. But first, you must understand the new marketplace. Just moving faster doesn't guarantee you're moving in the right direction. And you must acquire a deeper understanding of your marketplace. Be warned, it's much deeper than most marketers realize.

THE DIFFERENCE BETWEEN MARKETING AND ADVERTISING

WHY IT AND MATTERS

The word *marketing* has been misused so often there's hardly a real definition of it that's commonly understood. The word 'marketing' now seems to mean any number of things. It's often used as a synonym for sales, advertising, and other actions in the marketplace. Few people seem to understand the real meaning of marketing. But then, few people know the full meaning of advertising.

We've all heard people in businesses say they've hired a marketing representative when they've actually hired a salesperson. But I suppose marketing representative sounds more sophisticated even though it's wrong. Sophisticates often misspeak.

We commonly hear that someone is "marketing" a new product, when they mean they're selling a new product. Hopefully, they've already done the marketing for it, because marketing is done first, then advertising and selling are derived from a marketing plan.

People and companies that sell products in a marketplace are known as *marketers*. That name makes sense. It describes what they are.

The word *marketing* has a very strict definition and meaning to those who work in marketing. People like me. In this book, I use the word correctly because too much depends on clarity and understanding to play fast and loose with semantics and misused words.

A recent article by Daniel Burstein, writing for *Marketing Experiments*,[5] articulates the subject very well. So, allow me to excerpt some of his remarks.

---

[5] Excerpts from an article by Daniel Burstein of *Marketing Experiments* with his permission

First, he makes it clear that marketing and advertising and sales are not synonyms. So, let's examine the differences. Ponder the bigger, more existential elements of marketing. Marketing philosophy, as it were. It is not just words. Marketing is the overarching strategy that determines the means and efficacy of educating customers about their choices in the marketplace: for whom the marketer's product or service will be a good fit, and for whom it won't. Done correctly, we come away understanding who our prospective customers are and the reasons why.

Advertising is the execution of the marketing strategy to your target market group, or a segment within your target group. So, both advertising and marketing have the same goal. They both are essentially helping enable a choice to be made by the prospective customer in the company's favor to enable reaching a sales objective. And they both enable the best expression of a product or service to influence the decision for the customer, even if the best choice is not to purchase the company's products.

But there is a key difference between marketing and advertising. Each advertising effort is meant to only impact a segment of your target market with a defined benefit appealing to that specific targeted group. Even broad, multimedia, multichannel campaigns are designed to impact just a fraction of the customers with a brand. Done correctly, advertising addresses one distinction or benefit to one market, one segment at a time. Yes, it's possible to reach more prospects, but that's not the point. Addressing one segment with a distinct benefit to that segment is the only effective way to create a customer.

Advertising is not meant to be an attempt to include everything about the company and its products. It cannot be. Yet this is one of the biggest mistakes traditional marketers make. They're too focused on getting in front of the prospect or customer with the objective of making a sale. In so doing, they attempt to tell them everything about their product or service. But those who are contacted in this way won't respond. It's too much information. The prospect will be lost because of cognitive overload.

The question is not, "What is my objective as a marketer?" The question marketers should ask is, "What is my customer's objective?" And "How can I help them meet it with every customer contact?" That includes not only the actual product experience, but every experience with the customer, from advertising and sales, to customer service, to the return policy. This is the reason advertising must be a result of marketing (of your marketing plan), and why it cannot work alone. Remember this. It's critically important.

Burstein also says you should be your company's "chief customer experience officer," Which means, if it impacts the customer, it impacts the brand. And if it impacts the brand, it impacts purchase decisions, it impacts innovation, it impacts the very product itself, and it ultimately impacts the whole company in many more ways.

WHO WOULD HAVE THOUGHT?

YOU NEVER CHANGE THINGS BY FIGHTING
THE EXISTING REALITY.

—R. Buckminster Fuller

Buckminster Fuller was an architect, systems theorist, designer, and inventor. He thought outside the box long before "thinking outside the box" became a cliché. He was a great thinker. And that's where it all begins. Good-to-great results come from good-to-great thinking.

Buckminster Fuller conceived and built the geodesic dome. What a simple thing, really. But it's slap-you-in-the-face brilliant. Like great art, great music, and all great creations, its brilliance is in its simplicity; fastening triangles together adjacently, as many as you wish, and erecting them in the shape of a dome.

With no interior columns or other support, there is no limit to how large a geodesic dome can be. A geodesic dome can be made for a house, an office building (as Amazon has), to cover a huge sports stadium, or to cover a city, or . . . well, you get the idea.

Yet no matter how large, it will always carry its own weight; always hold itself up using the downward force of gravity on its own structural components. Imagine. Using gravity to hold a thing up. Think about that. Brilliant. Who would have thought? Well, Buckminster Fuller thought. And that's why I want to explore some of his thoughts a little more with you.

Consider Bucky's comment: "We are powerfully imprisoned by the terms in which we have been conducted to think." Meaning we must think beyond what we've been conditioned to think. Don't be "imprisoned" by the familiar. Keep your mind out on the edge, beyond the boundaries. Fight against the familiar, the preconceived ideas. They will only take you where you've already been.

Let's think about these "terms in which we have been conducted (conditioned) to think." They're also known as perceptions, but they're perceptions that have been created by external forces. The way the mind reacts to them are the "terms in which we've been conducted to think." They're tricky things.

"Conducted to think"? Psychologists would say, "conditioned to think." Conditioning is form of training. How we are trained by external forces, our experiences, and our internalized perceptions of the world is who we are. You see, if an idea, a perception, a perceived reality, is not already in the mind, the mind will fight you about it. The mind disdains new things. The mind hates change. It hates it when a thing is different than what it thinks (perceives) it is. So, the mind rejects it out of hand.

Human nature? No, it's deeper than that. Much deeper. And it's crucial to rethinking marketing. The tricky part, the inexplicable part of perceptions is that ten people can see the same thing and come away with ten different descriptions of what each saw (perceived). Because of this anomaly, police investigators will tell you that gathering "eyewitness" reports can be worthless. Remember the two friends in the flea market looking at the same chair.

So, the first thing we must know as marketers is that perceptions, the things that the mind is confined to, are the only things that matter. Perception is reality to the perceiver. Only perceptions matter. As a marketer, you must identify your prospects perceptions, and you must speak to them in your advertising and sales within their perceptions. For if you ignore their perceptions, they won't hear you because there will be no context and, therefore, no meaning for your message.

Perceptions are the mind's way of filtering ideas. They're the "ways we have been conducted or conditioned to think." They often take the form of an opinion. In fact, they're substantially the basis of an opinion. A person holding the opinion absolutely believes it's real and correct. Obviously, if this person didn't think it was true and real, then he or she wouldn't hold the opinion in the first place. This is the way in which perceptions are considered to be reality.

Sometimes perceptions are simply pigeonholing of experiences; sort of like a filing system of the mind to make it easier to comprehend the world. Our minds tells us that if something appears to be this, then it *is* this. There's an old saying: If it walks like a duck and quacks like a duck, then it's a duck. The mind may be dead wrong, but what it perceives is damned-well a duck. So, it doesn't matter whether it's really a duck at all, does it?

Amazing, isn't it? When I was young, just starting out in the world of marketing, and I first learned about this, I thought it was arrogance, intransigence, or being blatantly obtuse. But I was wrong. Really wrong. Don't make the same mistake. Perceptions are indeed reality, and that's that.

Perceptions can be a marketer's greatest tool. And perceptions can also be the greatest obstacle to communication. No matter how sensational the creativity of your advertising, or how clever the words are in your advertising, if it isn't attuned to your prospect's or customers' perceptions, then your message isn't reaching them. I see this constantly in TV and radio advertising. Many advertisers are trying to deliver their messages to too broad an audience. So broad that it's delivered to no one. Trying to be all things to all people means you're nothing to anybody. I often wonder who approves these advertisements, because, it's clear, they don't understand marketing or advertising.

Think of the Super Bowl ads everyone raves about. They're examples of great creativity and are cleverly done. People look forward to seeing them during the Super Bowl. So much so, they've become their own thing. There are even YouTube videos of them to watch later again and again. People love to watch these ads as entertainment. But these fun ads are seldom great advertising. You might instinctively disagree since they're so attention grabbing. Yes, they get our attention, but there must be more.

So, stop for a moment and think again. Presenting TV commercials almost purely for entertainment and a bit of "show-offishness" simply doesn't work as anything but brand awareness. And they may, indeed, reinforce awareness, but they rarely create sales. This is the reason so-called "branding" doesn't work well for a marketer. There's no accountability defining how many and who actually saw the ad, and who and how many were motivated to take action because of it.

The real question you should ask is: After the fun ends, how many products have these creative wonders sold? Studies show that the purchases of products advertised to Super Bowl viewers is "off-the-charts insignificant." Considering the huge audience that sees them, the response ought to also be huge. The response should be at least as much as the marketer's advertising creates elsewhere, if not better, since they're so clever. But that just isn't the case. Are they, as the British say, "Too clever by half"?

The provocative truth is perceptions are the most useful tool we have in marketing and in advertising and sales. And it's deeper than you may think. Perceptions born of emotion—emotional intelligence will cause prospects and customers to return again and again because an emotional engagement has been created with them.

Smart marketers push their success by using a simple method of communicating the essence of their business to the public: a clever way of maintaining top-of-mind awareness. And they will continue getting and keeping customers.

THE ASTOUNDING IMPORTANCE OF YOUR UNIQUE SELLING PROPOSITION

A POWERFUL MEANS OF KEEPING CUSTOMERS

We're bombarded with a continuous stream of sales talk and advertising coming from every imaginable source of auditory and visual stimuli. It's so much that most people stop hearing it. It's cognitive overload, and so viewers hit the off switch of the minds, or the mute button on their remote controls to retain sanity.

So, smart marketers use a *USP* (unique selling proposition). It's one of the most viable means for reaching through all this clutter to the prospects' and customers' minds with a quick message that will stick.

A unique selling proposition is a short statement that creates top-of-mind awareness by expressing an outstanding benefit in a memorable way.

But you can use a USP to position your company and its services only *if* you understand your customers and their needs. Remember the fellow who only thought he needed a drill, but really just needed holes? Understanding this means you understand your customers, and you understand engagement.

You must understand your customers to have an effective *USP*.

With a good *USP*, you can show your product's or service's unique benefit, a benefit that your customers are not getting now, and will not, or cannot, get from your competitors.

Here is a concise explanation for developing a *unique selling proposition* from an article by Will Swayne of *Marketing Results*:[6]

> In the mind of a potential client or customer, a USP defines the company's position in the market. It's a distinct and appealing idea that sets you apart from every other

---

[6] https://www.marketingresults.com.au/will-swayne/

"me too" competitor or alternative solution (including the alternative of doing nothing).

The USP places a product or service as unique and desirable in the eyes of prospects and customers to create top-of-mind awareness.

The USP is an essential part of the foundation of a marketing strategy. Every company that wants to be successful must have a clear USP. It's imperative.

There is a caveat, however: a great USP with average execution can succeed, but a weak USP even with superb execution usually fails.

To create your own USP, you must ask and answer the following questions:

- What are the strengths and weaknesses of your competitors?
- Why do repeat clients and customers like your product?
- What makes you better than your competitors?

If you can answer these questions, you can develop a USP. You already know what makes your company different and better, but you must communicate this to your prospects. It takes a little time to develop a USP, but the upside is that there's no cost to it.

(Note: The USP is particularly important for digital marketing, websites, etc. It should be the primary attention grabber of a website landing page. But it must be good.)

One of the major benefits of a strong USP is that it can help you stay out of a price war. Yes, some people shop purely for price and "the absolute lowest prices." Can you imagine that? But when you position yourself correctly, you can even charge more.

For example, let's say you're in the public golf course business, which can be extremely competitive. You're in a suburb and there are five golf courses near yours, so there's always a brutal price war going on, and you'd like to get out of the battle. You know that golfers always comment on the quality of the greens at a golf course, so, a strong USP could be:

"Rolling Hills Country Club has the best greens in the South Ridgewood area."

Golfers value great putting surfaces and would be willing to pay more for a course with excellent greens.

Another situation calls for a different approach. In the New York City area, where golf can be funereally slow, especially on weekends, one course guarantees "a round of golf in four hours or less, or your next green fee is on us." They can do this and charge more for it because they're good managers of the flow of golfers at the start of the course. The result is that it's a highly successful USP. And a highly successful golf course.

Before we go any further, note this: A USP is not a tagline or slogan, and a tagline or slogan is not a USP. A tagline is a short sentence or phrase that's often part of a company's logo or next to it. A tagline is usually too short to communicate your entire USP.

However, there is value in a great tagline in that it can quickly summarize the full USP and communicates the key selling proposition at a glance—usually in one or two seconds. Think of how this can improve a website visitor's engagement, since the typical viewer's time viewing a new website is under four seconds before the viewer decides to move on not having found anything of interest.

So, a USP can be a few words, or it can be a full paragraph expressing in a brief summary what makes you different, unique, and desirable.

This is more important than the number of words. Even if it's a full paragraph, don't believe the falsehood that no one will read that much. People who are interested will read it. (If they aren't interested, then they won't be looking at it in the first place.)

Remember: a successful USP answers this question: Why should a potential client or customer buy from you? When answering this question, promise something special that your competitors cannot deliver. Something that makes you distinct and memorable.

Just as some taglines are poor, many USPs are awful. The following examples are too vague. Plus, they aren't unique:

- "Good Quality and Low Prices"
- "Affordable Quality Since 1984"

- "Service with A Smile"
- "Excellence in Quality and Service"

These USPs are commonplace. What do they really say? They seem to say: these companies have nothing of specific value to sell.

Here are the two parts for creating a bulletproof USP.

1) USPs are grouped into one of these categories:

- price
- quality
- service
- speed
- selection
- convenience
- guarantee
- customization
- originality
- specialization

2) To create a definite and precise form and communicate your unique strengths, ask yourself these four questions:

1) What do you offer that your competitors don't?
2) Is being number one important to your customers?
3) How easy is it for competitors to copy?
4) Can it be communicated easily?

These concepts are broad. For example, if you choose 'Service' as your category, you have to say more and be more specific than "We Have *Great* Service." This kind of cliché won't convince anyone to do anything.

In the seventies, Avis car rental had been operating for years at a loss. Avis's board hired Robert Townsend, a well-known turnaround guy, as their new CEO because they were struggling. (The word *struggling* vastly understates their condition since they hadn't made a profit in thirteen years.)

Townsend was brilliant. He knew he had to come up with a totally new approach to the marketplace to gain a desperately needed market advantage and to increase their market share. And of course, to turn a profit. Or, at the very least, not lose more money. He said they needed a unique selling proposition, a USP that was very powerful. After all, Hertz was well ahead of them in size and market share.

What did he do? Working with Bill Bernbach, then one of the most creative minds in the marketing and advertising world, they came up with a masterful positioning concept, and it became their unique selling proposition: "We're number two. So, we try harder." The uniqueness was in the fact that they publicly admitted their place in the rental car business. It was effective because of the claim it made—publicly admitting Avis was not number one. It was not so-called "reverse psychology." It was simply shockingly honest.

The upshot was that even though they still rented cars as they always had just like Hertz, they positioned themselves as the company that would work harder and give better service and better rates, because they would try harder to please customers and get some new customers in the bargain. And they made incredible progress and growth because of this single USP, a market position they established by heavily advertising it to the public. Both existing customers and new customers saw this and heard it.

So, what happened? After this positioning concept was introduced into their marketplace, Avis business and sales increased so much that, for the first time in thirteen years, Avis made a profit.

Now this USP is a classic. Avis's unique selling proposition that created their market position entered prospect's and customer's minds so extraordinarily well that the phrase entered the public lexicon. The slogan became a generic expression, a humorous answer for anyone struggling to do anything. It lasted for years.

Companies have slogans taken from their USP for the same reason they have logos as a visual representation of a brand. Slogans are audible representations of a brand. They're easier to remember. Hopefully, if a prospect remembers nothing else from an advertisement, they'll remember the slogan. And they will remember the product by association.

Here is a list of words or phrases that have created top-of-mind awareness for some of the world's biggest advertisers.

1) Nike: "Just Do It"
2) Apple: "Think Different"
3) Dollar Shave Club: "Shave Time. Shave Money."
4) L'Oréal: "Because You're Worth It"
5) California Milk Processor Board: "Got Milk?"
6) MasterCard: "There are some things money can't buy. For everything else, there's MasterCard."
7) BMW: "The Ultimate Driving Machine"
8) Tesco: "Every Little Helps"
9) M&M: "Melts in Your Mouth, Not in Your Hands"
10) Bounty: "The Quicker Picker Upper"
11) De Beers: "A Diamond is Forever"
12) Lay's: "Betcha Can't Eat Just One"
13) Audi: "Advancement Through Technology"
14) Dunkin' Donuts: "America Runs on Dunkin"
15) Meow Mix: "Tastes So Good, Cats Ask for It by Name
16) McDonald's: "I'm Lovin' It"
17) *The New York Times*: "All the News That's Fit to Print"
18) General Electric: "Imagination at Work"
19) Verizon: "Can You Hear Me Now? Good."
20) State Farm: "Like a Good Neighbor, State Farm is There."
21) Maybelline: "Maybe she's born with it. Maybe it's Maybelline."
22) The US Marine Corps: "The Few. The Proud. The Marines."

I'll bet you recall almost every slogan and the product it represents. That's the power of mnemonics.

We've discovered perceptions' linkage with emotions. Next, we'll discover perceptions of groups of people and how we can use this to our advantage in the marketplace. It's fascinating.

PERCEPTIONS HELD BY GROUPS OF PEOPLE MARKETERS CANNOT POSSIBLY DEAL WITH EVERY INDIVIDUAL'S PERCEPTION.

BUT WE CAN DEAL WITH GROUPS HAVING SIMILAR PERCEPTIONS.

Perceptions held by groups of people are the primary things you're dealing with in marketing. How well you communicate with those groups holding these perceptions will govern your success.

The psychology of groups has kept me endlessly fascinated. People and groups of people keep us connected to the deeper elements of marketing as well as the broader facets of our society and culture. People create the organic marketplace, and people are what makes it act and react, keeping it in motion. As we rethink marketing, we also rethink the fundamental ideas driving people—prospects and customers. Their emotions and perceptions.

Think of it like this. Businesses really don't sell products, services, or even expertise; businesses sell satisfaction. Here's one example: "XYZ Company sells car insurance, but that's almost secondary. What XYZ Company really sells is comfort: the comfort of knowing that if you have an accident, they will take care of your loss."

Great salespeople don't try to sell things. Instead, they connect with their prospects and customers through emotion—appealing to those feelings valued by customers and who or what they want to be. Great salespeople simply enable customers to buy things.

Even though you're appealing to a group, always create your message as if it is speaking to one person, the person who reads it or hears it. All effective advertising is personal. Every person who sees or hears your communication in any form must feel as though it is speaking directly to him or her personally. The next time you're in the audience at a seminar or conference, you'll remember who the best speakers were—that is, those whom you paid the closest attention and learned the most because you felt they directly, even personally, connected with you.

The best, most effective public speakers know the art of this. In any speech or presentation, they'll look at a single person as they complete a sentence. Then to another person for the next sentence, holding that person with their eyes for the complete sentence. At the end, most all the people in the audience will feel that the speaker was talking directly to them personally. People remember this speaker with warmth as if they know him or her personally. Try it the next time you make a speech or presentation. You'll be electrified by the reception of your listeners.

Marketing is about the larger scheme of things, the perceptions of people in groups. In advertising, people in groups are generally predictable if you know the reasons your customers' respond to your business's offering. If not, there could be no such thing as advertising.

However, the actions of a single individual are not predictable even if that person is a friend or relative. A person's perception is just that; one person's perception. So, trying to predict an individual's actions is simply guessing what such a person might do or might think.

Yet there are enough people with similar perceptions of the world (they don't need to be *exactly* the same) that we as marketers can generally define our market group. Said another way, the group is our marketplace. The more people with similar perceptions about our product or service, the larger our group and the larger our marketplace.

Perceptions among groups don't dilute perceptions. In fact, it tends to create more impetus and momentum, and a more broadly understood identity of a product. This is what we're building toward. It's very useful knowledge for you in your marketplace.

Incidentally, there are several ways to succeed in big markets that are so big a business can get lost in them. We'll discuss them in depth later when we talk about segmentation, categories, niche markets, submarkets, and positioning by distinction.

Politics illustrates an interesting view of the perception of groups. Political advertising and all such public political communications purposely and directly strives to pit one perception against another to split or divide groups into two or more ways of perceiving a thing. Dividing groups is an aggressive action, and it reveals hardcore, emotionally driven perceptions with a take-no-prisoners attitude. Groups of people will vote, or advocate, a certain way. And another group will advocate in a different, if not opposite, way. The beliefs that groups advocate are the perceptions that they have in common with other advocates about their candidate, their issue, and their ideology.

These are closely held perceptions, and the group is so emotionally tied to them they expand them beyond logic. Such groups will ignore variances in the details to maintain the larger perception. We've all seen this during any election and special issue voting.

Even now, political groups have become quite divided over ideas and ideologies that have not been historically divisive. Indeed, these groups have become very aggressive in their attitudes. Behavior follows belief. It's an excellent illustration of the phenomenon of group psychology.

Here's a quote from Sigmund Freud's *Group Psychology and the Analysis of the Ego*:

> A group is extraordinarily credulous and open to influence. It has no critical faculty. Anyone who wishes to produce an effect upon it needs no logical adjustment to his arguments; he must paint in the most forcible colors, he must exaggerate, and he must repeat the same thing again and again. The group respects force and can only be slightly influenced by kindness, which it regards merely as a form of weakness. It wants to be ruled and oppressed, and to fear its masters. And finally, groups have never thirsted after truth. They demand illusions and cannot do without them. They constantly give what is unreal precedence over what is real; they are almost as strongly influenced by what is untrue as by what is true. They have an evident tendency not to distinguish between the two. A group is an obedient herd, which could never live without a master. It has such a thirst for obedience that it submits instinctively to anyone who appoints himself as its master.

Freud is often called the "father of modern psychology." While his core ideas were not incorrect, the ideas he expressed here as "group psychology" are more like crowd psychology, which Freud describes as *mob psychology*. This points up the differences and the similarities between group psychology and mob psychology, given that psychology is not an exact science.

You might enjoy reading the book *Extraordinary Popular Delusions and the Madness of Crowds*, an early study of crowd psychology by Charles MacKay, published in 1841. I think you'll find it captivating. It provides a long perspective of the actions of people in groups, and the compelling idea that people don't change. Times change, but we find that people's needs, motivation, and ideas have remained the same regardless of the passage of time or of the context.

The Power of Shared Group Perceptions

J. K. Rowling is a household name. Her stories about Harry Potter have sold more than 450-million books and have become part of our culture. Every Harry Potter book she publishes becomes an instant bestseller. Movies are made from them. Her books and stories are translated into other languages and loved everywhere by both children and adults.

A while back, a detective novel was written, titled *The Cuckoo's Calling*, by an unknown writer named Robert Galbraith. It had mixed success. People who read it said it was "engaging" and "inspired." Unfortunately, there weren't very many people who had read it, so it languished on bookstore shelves, selling only fifteen hundred hardcover copies in three months. Then one day *The Cuckoo's Calling* blew the doors off and jumped from number 4,709 to the number one best-selling book on Amazon.com. Hundreds of thousands of copies were sold.

Was Robert Galbraith suddenly discovered to be a genius? Not at all. And a closer inspection of the book showed that it wasn't really a literary masterpiece. There was nothing extraordinary about *The Cuckoo's Calling*. It was just another one of many well-written mystery books on the market. But when someone found out that Robert Galbraith was a pen name used by J. K. Rowling, word spread like wildfire. With that, the perception of *The Cuckoo's Calling* changed in the blink of an eye.

That's the power of group perceptions shared. And of the built-in credibility of perceptions.

Next is a follow-up to the psychology of groups. It's a scientific study about how completely normal people can be pressured into unusual behavior by the consensus around them. It may astound you.

THE ASCH EXPERIMENT COMPLETELY NORMAL PEOPLE CAN BE PRESSURED INTO UNUSUAL BEHAVIOR BY THE CONSENSUS AROUND THEM.

The Asch experiment, conducted by Solomon Asch in the 1950s, is one of a famous series of landmark studies to test how peer pressure influences the judgment and individuality of people.[7] The results can then be projected into the general population within calculations of error factors and confidence levels, which I won't go into here for fear of rendering you stupefied or unconscious.

The Asch experiment is related closely to the Stanford prison and Milgram experiments in that its thesis was to show how ordinary, normally functioning human beings can be pressured into unusual behavior by authority figures or by the consensus of opinion around them.

(During the war crimes trials at Nuremberg, Germany, after World War II, Nazi concentration camp guards and commandants on trial as war criminals said with sincerity, they were only following orders. They honestly thought this was an acceptable reason and believed it absolved them of any crime.)

For the Asch experiment, eight subjects were seated around a table, with the seating plan carefully constructed to prevent any suspicion that could affect outcomes. Only one participant was a genuine subject for the experiment, the rest were shills, confederates carefully tutored to give certain preselected responses. Careful experimental construction placed a varying amount of peer pressure on the single, individual test subject.

---

[7] Note: There are many studies and observations that prove to us that people's basic self-referencing attitudes don't change. This study was conducted in the 1950s, but it will never be out-of-date. People's attitudes, actions and reactions are timeless. Any study of history shows this to be obvious.

The experiment was simple in its construction; each participant, in turn, was asked to answer a series of questions, such as which line on a piece of paper was longest, or which line matched a reference line also on the paper. The participants gave a variety of answers, at first correct, to avoid arousing suspicion in the subject, but then later some incorrect responses were added. This would allow Asch to determine how the answers of the test subject would change with the added influence of peer pressure.

The Asch experiment results were astonishing. They clearly showed that peer pressure could have a measurable influence on the answers given. The control group, those not exposed to peer pressure where everybody gave correct answers, had only one incorrect response out of 35; this single incorrect response could probably be explained by experimental error.

The results for the other groups were interesting. When surrounded by people giving an incorrect answer, over one-third of the subjects also voiced an incorrect opinion. At least 75 percent of the subjects gave the wrong answer to at least one question. Again, experimental error may have had some influence on this figure. There was no doubt, however, that peer pressure was causing conformity. It was debated whether this is because people disbelieve the evidence of their own eyes, or if it was just for compliance that people hide their opinions.

Follow-ups to the Asch experiment showed that the number of dissenting voices made a difference to the results, just as the forcefulness of the confederates also made a difference. One incorrect confederate made little difference to the answers, but the influence steadily increased if two or three people disagreed.

Fascinating, isn't it? We can all be swayed in our perceptions by those around us. And this is particularly true if some of those around us are forceful in their ideas, perceptions, and opinions. This is quite common and helps us understand the power and suasion of groups.

This is leads me to discuss the use of focus groups.

You probably know about focus groups. Certain news and current event TV programs use them "live" on the program to determine a consensus about a subject. However, even though focus groups are used by some TV news organizations to offer instantaneous answers on the air to public policy questions, they're very weak in credibility.

I don't use focus groups for primary research. A group can be swayed too easily by forceful opinions expressed by other participants that are especially aggressive. This is especially true if the focus group is dealing with a divisive opinion or attitude; the way someone views a thing or behaves toward it. Having a professional moderator is a must and is always advised, but the aggression displayed by some individuals will disrupt the group's focus, overwhelming the purpose of the focus group.

Even though one can screen participants for this disruptive attitude, underlying attitudes of overbearing personality types can be hidden, not apparent during a screening only to appear later in the focus group as a disruption. Conflicts can be helpful in parsing ideas; putting a finer point on a thing, but when they devolve to arguing and even shouting, as I've witnessed, then they distort the study and render the findings worthless.

I strongly advise against using focus groups for any reason. Far too many product and service attributes are negatively influenced or misunderstood because of unfounded conflicts among participants of focus groups. This phenomenon will skew the determined results and misinform and cause misunderstanding about the product or service being investigated. As the owner and account manager of an advertising agency, I refuse to use a client's money for a thing that cannot be confirmed with complete credibility.

GROUP PERCEPTIONS OUTSIDE YOUR CULTURE

THERE ARE VAST CULTURAL DIFFERENCES IN PERCEPTIONS BETWEEN THE AMERICAN (US) CULTURE AND EVERY OTHER CULTURE IN THE WORLD.

Culture can make an unforgiving difference to you if your consumer is from a culture unlike the American culture. I lived for several years in the Far East, a very different culture than that of the United States. For my part, it required some effort and objectivity and courtesy to assimilate into that culture as much as possible. That's not to say that anyone ever mistook me for anything but an American. Yet I got along well with the people because I made a genuine attempt to understand them personally, as well as a society, and as a culture. I found they appreciated and respected that. Yet, this is not a great finding. It's only empathy and a willingness to trust shown in a common-sense way.

I've been to a lot of places in the world, and I've found this to be true everywhere. It genuinely flatters people to know that I care enough to ask about their country and society. I can say, without reservation, that people's emotional wants and needs are basically the same anywhere and everywhere in the world. Yet the perceptions they hold are very different and must be understood within the context of their culture, their history, their religion, their environment, and their experience.

It would require another book to describe this. A very large book. An anthropology book would be a good start. But only a start. So, I won't go into this in detail since it is too vast to describe every cultural idiosyncrasy and nuance, I've experienced. Here's why. And this may surprise you. It amazed me.

Did you know that we are culturally conditioned to perceive color? This is fascinating. But there's even more. Would you imagine that Eskimos have seventeen words for "white" as it applies to snow conditions? As I said, it absolutely amazed me.

So how can you deal with that? You don't, because you can't, unless you're Inuit. And if you are, then you already knew it, and it's no big deal.

My suggestion is that if you find yourself needing to communicate (to advertise) in a different culture, be very circumspect. Perceptions are most assuredly not the same.

It's an absolute rule that one must be cautiously specific to the culture. I'd advise you to find a person from a specific culture for a guide and adviser. If you want to advertise in France, don't just talk to a European. Talk to a French person. Maybe several because their answers will vary depending on what part of France they live in.

I once put myself in a situation that demanded my chastisement while having a drink with some friends in France when I compared cognac with Armagnac, which is a very specific "cognac" from southern France. The French take their cuisine and their beverages very seriously. Don't ever forget it. Another lesson learned.

Another reminder that perceptions are not the same between cultures. So, one must be very careful because there are many ways a simple sentence, phrase, or even a word can be translated depending on the intent of the user, the user's native language, and the dialect in that language. It's very complex.

I learned that even within an Eastern culture, many of the people native to that culture are hesitant to translate a piece written by another because they have no way of knowing the intent of the writer. The emphasis, tone, and even the context and various usages of a word or phrase make a difference about the writer's intent.

And more. Just because most of our ancestors came from Europe, Africa, and Latin America, the perceptions within the American culture compared with these cultures have striking differences. Don't take any similarity on its face, or you'll rue the day.

The very way we in America think about ourselves and others, and even the way we perceive reality, makes us distinct from other people in the world, distinct even from the vast majority of our ancestors. Don't misunderstand. The American culture is not better or worse than any other. But it is distinctly different.

Among Westerners, studies show that Americans are often the most unusual. This led researchers to conclude that Americans are an exception even among Westerners; outliers among outliers.

The Western mind, specifically the American mind, is the most self-aggrandizing and egotistical on the planet. That's not a value judgment; it's just a fact. We are more likely to promote ourselves as individuals versus advancing as a group. This has deep ramifications for Americans communicating within other cultures. Even among Western cultures, American minds are more analytic and tend to focus in on an object of interest rather than understanding that object in the context of what is around it.

It's also important to know that cultures are not monolithic. Even the American culture can be endlessly parsed. Ethnic backgrounds, religious beliefs, economic status, parenting styles, rural upbringing versus urban, or suburban. There are hundreds of cultural differences that exist individually and in endless combinations influencing our concepts of fairness, how we categorize things, our method of judging and decision making, and our deeply held beliefs about the nature of the self among other aspects of our psychological makeup.

Cultural anthropologists say they're just beginning to learn how these fine-grained cultural differences affect our thinking. Recent research has shown that people in "tight" cultures, those with strong norms and low tolerance for deviant behavior (think India, Malaysia, Pakistan, China) develop higher impulse control and more self-monitoring abilities than those from other places.

This was quite noticeable when I lived in the Far East and in India. Exuberance is somewhat shocking to people in this culture. And that was a major hurdle for me to overcome. Being excitable is thought of as a loss of self-control. In America, it's quite the opposite and is generally seen as enthusiasm. I'm quite excitable. It adds to the fun of life. But it doesn't translate well.

Research published recently noted psychological differences at the city level too. I've noticed this to be profound within the American culture as I'm sure you have too. Compared to San Franciscans, Bostonians' sense of self-worth is more dependent on ancestry, community status, and financial and educational achievement. San Franciscans tend to base their self-worth on open-mindedness and that they're somewhat removed from others. I've had clients in both cities, and I've become starkly aware of these differences.

Can a rural middle-class person from Mississippi have a meaningful conversation with a middle-class person from Massachusetts? Dialect alone would be a nearly insurmountable obstacle, not to mention the lack of shared societal perceptions.

If human cognition is shaped by cultural ideas and behavior, it can't be studied without considering what those ideas and behaviors are, and how they're different from place to place. Cultural psychology comparing Western and Eastern concepts of the self, goes to the heart of this question. Think small now. Such differences may be the results of cultural activities and trends going back thousands of years.

Whether you think of yourself as interdependent or independent may depend on whether your distant ancestors farmed rice (which required a great deal of shared labor and group cooperation) or herded animals (which rewarded individualism and aggression). That's very interesting. It seems to suggest that much of our psychological makeup is inherited, genetically.

Cultural anthropologists have found another salient marker; the analytic verses holistic dichotomy in reasoning styles can be clearly seen between Greek (Western) and Chinese (Eastern) philosophical writing dating back 2,500 years. I'd say this makes a strong case, not to be treated lightly.

This reinforces the underlying power of perceptions. What has been discussed here illustrates why the marketplace is organic, almost a living thing, since it exists within the living interactions among people—people in other cultures and parts of the world.

Psychologically and sociologically, people, societies, and cultures are in a constant state of change. During the past few hundred years, this is happening faster because of more outside influences impacting them (the internet for one, ease of travel for another) than at any time in history.

MOTIVATIONS AND BARRIERS

YOU CANNOT CHANGE THINGS BY
FIGHTING THE EXISTING REALITY.
—R. Buckminster Fuller (again)

An existing reality is a perception existing in people's minds. Delving into perceptions of people in groups reveals the most likely motivators, as well as the most likely barriers to motivation.

Begin by striving to understand the perceptions people hold of your competitors' product or service. If that's done right, then we're close to understanding the perceptions they will most likely hold of similar products and services, that is to say, of your product or service.

We've discussed this earlier, but here we see it in a different context. Think of it like this. Your competitors wouldn't be competitors if they didn't have a product/service that's very similar to yours. So, this means your prospects are found within your competitors' customers. This is your marketplace, and these people are your prospects. Reach them and do your job well and many of them will become *your* customers.

The more you work at creating the perception of your product as being similar to your more well-known competitors, but perceived to have better benefits, notable innovations and enticingly different points of distinction, the better chance you have of gaining new customers and increasing your share of the marketplace.

Hold this thought while we revisit Buckminster Fuller's profound observation setting up the next thing we will consider. He's talking about introducing something new. Geodesic domes maybe. But we can apply his thoughts to marketing and learn from him.

> You never change things by fighting the existing reality.
> To change something, a mind perhaps, build a new model
> that makes the existing model obsolete.

This is a major insight; a warning. Because if you fight existing reality, it's a fight you'll almost always lose. The mind disdains new things. Creating new perceptions of a thing does not change a mind, but it's the first step. This is the beginning of understanding people and our marketplace. We understand that the mind does not easily accept new things. The mind remains skeptical and unbelieving of a new thing. I'm sure you've noticed that.

Skepticism is a healthy and instinctive reaction to new things. It's kept the human species alive since the first person learned that crawling out on a weak branch and falling out of his tree could mean death from the predators waiting below. The fewer who made that mistake, or learned from it, the more who survived. And so here we are, still surviving using our instincts, and our instincts tell us to not readily accept new things, or we could fall out of our tree, figuratively speaking of course.

We can call it skepticism, distrust, apprehension, disbelieving—anything that causes people to be risk averse. Anything "new" is perceived to be a risk. In our deep primal brains (the hypothalamus), risk equates with possible death. We are programmed, hardwired to survive, so risk of death is a thing we instinctively avoid without conscious thought. It's risk aversion. We ignore our ancient instincts at our own peril.

One cannot change minds, but one can change perceptions carefully by engagement. Indeed, we can change perceptions of anything, and done skillfully, lead people to change their own minds because they want to. So, as Bucky advises, we must create a different model with some modifications such that it continues to overlay existing perceptions.

This is the process of changing perceptions to fit what is already in the minds of our prospects and customers. It's the launching pad of advertising. So, run from conventional thinking like your hair is on fire.

DEVELOPING AN ADVERTISING PLAN

YOU'VE GOT TO BE VERY CAREFUL IF YOU
DON'T KNOW WHERE YOU ARE GOING,
BECAUSE YOU MIGHT NOT GET THERE.

—Yogi Berra

An advertising plan cannot be created until one has a marketing plan. And advertising is never done without an advertising plan. Your advertising is the implementation of your marketing plan. It reflects the information of your marketing plan, and tells you exactly what to do, how to do it, and when to do it, and with whom (i.e., your market segment).

It's crucial to know your prospects and customers as well as you know your product or service. Together, the interaction or cooperation of two or more things produce a combined effect greater than the sum of their separate effects. It's called *synergy*. This enables the best communication with your prospects and customers. So, they must be the major part of your marketing plan and of your advertising plan.

Your advertising might use the mediums of TV, radio, newspapers, billboards, magazines, the internet, social media, websites, blogs—the usual things we think of when we hear the term, but it can take other forms too. Direct sales, direct mail, point of purchase sales (the lifeblood of convenience stores), and more.

We've even used skywriting and gigantic hot-air balloons. Yeah, some of the crazy stuff I mentioned earlier. The thing is, these crazy things worked, but obviously, there are very few instances when a hot-air balloon is the best tactic. And hardly any for skywriting.

These bizarre methods of advertising were tactics we used to create awareness and dominance of a new radio station in a very competitive radio market among more than a dozen Top 40 radio stations. That these worked makes more sense now, doesn't it?

Tactics are the things that make the cash register ring in a manner of speaking. That's the way Top 40 radio was back in the day. They had to do crazy things to get the attention of their primary listener demographic—people ages twelve to eighteen and ages eighteen to thirty-four—in a market packed with radio stations.

The point is that every advertising tactic is always led by a strictly construed advertising plan, which is directly derived from your marketing plan. Never from anything else. If you advertise and make it up as you go along, you'll waste money and generally be unsuccessful. That's a polite way of saying it doesn't work. Always follow the plan.

Advertising works well when it's done well. We have only to look around us to see how advertising shapes our world. Its powers of persuasion can't be ignored. Advertising influences our decisions and even the way we see and understand our world. Our perceptions.

The power of advertising has had a great effect on the ideas and cultural mores of our society. That may not be all for the good, but it's true. Advertising is the driving force of the marketplace and much of the popular culture. It's one of our society's greatest 'connecters'.

Those of us who work in the craft understand this because we see the results: the studies, the surveys, and the decision making and purchases of those we affect.

The power of the imagery and the message employed comes from understanding your prospects and customers and their perceptions of your product's marketplace which, of course, includes your competitors as well.

This is the reason and the purpose for having a great marketing plan. Advertising cannot be considered, much less done well, or even correctly, without the information you have in your marketing plan.

GETTING AND KEEPING CUSTOMERS IS THE ONLY PURPOSE OF A BUSINESS

AND IT REQUIRES THOUGHT AND HARD WORK

Condensed to its essence, marketing is everything you must do to influence the public, to find your prospects, and then to turn them into customers by causing them to feel personal, emotional reasons they should buy your offering. Thus, getting new customers. At least once.

But then you must keep them. And that requires thought and work. The role of salespeople and selling is changing very fast. This is one more reason to rethink marketing and to stay abreast of our new fast-moving marketplace. By 2020, the customer will manage eighty percent of his or her relationship with an enterprise without interacting with a human.

Salespeople have traditionally been the first step in a purchase process. They have been the customer's first point of contact with a company. So, they have significant power to influence customers' decision-making by controlling information about pricing, availability, competitive advantage, and so on.

But the marketplace is changing fast. We now live and work in an environment of nearly ubiquitous information. Information is everywhere. That means customers usually engage with salespeople after they've already researched their choices of products and, in many cases, after they have already made their purchase decision.

Many consumers question the importance of having a personal sales relationship at all. Most of the time, they know what they want and so they buy it—online without interacting with a single real person.

This is a critical issue for getting and keeping customers. In the new marketplace success isn't predicated on the number or size of sales. It's measured by getting and keeping the *right* customers.

Much to the surprise of a lot of people, intellectual reasons don't motivate anyone to do anything. As we understand people and the process, you'll see that emotions are the real motivators. Perceptions are reality, and they're emotional in origin.

Be aware that there are also emotional barriers to motivation. So, it's not just a matter of jumping through hoops and over hurdles to emotionally motivate your prospect. It's about knowing and understanding your prospects and customers. That's the context, and we're about to discover the single most important strategic means of getting and keeping the *right* customers.

Marketing is about engagement, meaning relationships. Perceptions create the beginning of relationships. Your emotional IQ is very important for this. Don't ignore it.

All relationships come with expectations of intimacy and trust. Understanding your prospects' and customers' perceptions is crucial.

Trust is big, really big for instilling intimacy.

Empathy may be a better word for the emotion that causes your prospect to feel a close association with your business and product. Empathy is always a large part of any relationship.

It's so large some marketers cannot grasp it because of a lack of emotional intelligence. Big business doesn't stand a chance unless these behemoths develop expert customer-relations tools and are sincere about them. And, additionally, the customer must recognize it, feel it. But very few big businesses are presently acting on this because they can't provide the empathy necessary.

Intimacy by way of empathy goes a long way in building trust. Trust isn't automatically given. There are too many charlatans and liars in the marketplace. So, trust must be earned and demonstrated by your process of engagement.

Engagement is a process, and it takes more time than many are willing to give. So, they will gain very few new customers in our new marketplace because they don't get it. And it doesn't matter how smart you are. Success doesn't come from having great intelligence. Believe it or not, most of the successful small business owners I know were B and C level college students. Some are only high school graduates.

Don't misunderstand me to say that smart, intelligent people aren't, or won't be, successful. But I truly know that real success ultimately comes from having astoundingly good emotional intelligence; empathizing with the way your customers and prospects perceive their needs. That's what relationships are built on. Nothing else.

The best salespeople I know are just simply good with people. They have an advantage – a natural inborn sense of emotional intelligence.

Their secret, if there is one, is that good salespeople are always working at creating a relationship, not just a transaction. They want to keep their customers coming back, and engagement is the process. Relationships are one of the deepest and most important elements to getting and keeping customers. And it's especially important in our currently fast-paced marketing environment.

As I mentioned earlier, the marketplace is organic, dynamic, and it has natural laws. I'm repeating what I've said before because it's important to remember that every market intrinsically reacts the same. That doesn't mean the problem solving is easier. It means the only affects you can have on it are what you do and don't do. And how you do it. Working directly with customers will give you the context for this.

One of the best pieces of advice I got before starting my own business was to work as a salesperson in a retail store for two years. I was told this would teach me about "selling" and working with people firsthand. I took the advice. It was very good advice, and I learned a lot. I would even suggest it to you.

ℴℂ

Several years ago, Dr. Theodore Levitt, the well-known and well-regarded professor of marketing at Harvard Business School, wrote many profound and outstanding papers, articles, and books about marketing. One book I gained a lot from reading was titled *The Marketing Imagination*. In this book, he stressed one simple core theme: "the purpose of a business is to get and keep customers." If that's accepted and understood, then everything else you're striving for will follow.

His book became quite well-known in the business community. It was another 'aha moment' for many people because it's foundational to everything you must do to be successful. And it's a key element of what I hope you take from this book.

You see, it doesn't matter what business you're in because every market presents the same kinds of challenges and requires the same efforts and the same kinds of solutions. If this were not true, then there could be no such thing as an advertising agency, which has a myriad of clients, each with a different product or service to sell. People's reaction to purchasing has many strategic and tactical common denominators

Dr. Levitt advised his readers to forget about all the wonderful sounding mission statements and the self-aggrandizing falderal accompanying these feel-good things. What is a mission statement but a list of things you'd like your customers to believe you do, or aspire to do? And they all say virtually the same things. Think about it. It assumes the customer must be told what the business does for them, or can do, or intends to do. In many ways it's condescending.

They're worthless as an internal message as well. Ask yourself: Could your mission statement actually make your business *un*distinctive? The thinking behind this question is that if you believe you need to tell your prospects and customers what you're prepared to do for them, then a sameness appears about your company when it's compared to others, and that makes your company anything but distinctive.

Prospects and customers evaluate your business in many ways depending on their needs and wants. I guarantee a mission statement is not one of ways they evaluate your business. It means nothing to them. Make your product and service offerings distinctive from your competitors, and you can and will get and keep customers. And your mission statement has nothing to do with it.

If your business is not distinctive in its marketplace, then it's invisible. Be convinced that the *purpose* of your business is "to get and keep customers." Write your business's purpose on a piece of paper and hang it up on the wall in place of your mission statement. That will do more for you and your people than a mission statement. And customers may even like it for its unusually fresh and honest approach. You know, being customers and all, they appreciate it.

Any advertising effort may get customers once. But keeping those hard-earned customers requires thinking differently. Marketing and advertising is a *long-term*, ongoing effort for matching your business's *long-term* needs and goals with those of your prospects' and customers' long-term needs and goals. Please go back to the definition of the word *marketing* and read it again. It's really that important.

Your new and existing customers know your product and service, so they're the most likely to do business with your company again. Existing customers are your greatest asset. In fact, they're exactly the value and worth of your business and not a penny less. Without customers, your tangible assets are worth nothing.

Keeping customers is the most critical issue facing any business. It would seem obvious that it's much less costly to keep customers once you have acquired them than to have to constantly seek out and acquire new customers, which is the only other alternative. Reinventing the wheel every day is not a long-term strategy.

Lack of knowing the value of existing customers is a reason that many businesses fail. Customers don't grow on trees. And they don't like being taken for granted. This is the primary reason for the big stores in shopping malls going broke.

The farther we get into this, the easier it is to understand why this new marketplace has arisen. Consumers aren't going to accept the uncaring treatment found with most retailers. They're tired of it, and they're not going to take it anymore. They're going elsewhere — have gone elsewhere.

Getting and keeping customers by engagement with an expectation of intimacy and trust goes a long way toward creating perceptions and emotions that are the real deal with a new consumer.

Getting new customers and keeping them means we must listen to our customers and nurture them towards a mutually desired outcome with trust. Remember: trust is earned and built.

A common mistake made by too many marketers is only paying attention to prospects who are ready to buy immediately but pay little attention to those who like the service or product, have thought about buying for a while, but are not quite ready for a variety of reasons to make a buying decision.

Not every prospect can be sold immediately. There are many definitions of a prospect. And many kinds of prospects with a variety of shades and textures. They're people, and they have their own lives to live. Your product or service may not be the most important thing to them right now. Yet every prospect is a prospective customer.

Prospects progress toward a business or product or service at their own pace. Prospects are your future customers. Every business must have a long line of prospects—future customers moving toward it.

So, keep them in the loop. Work hard to continue communicating with them. Cause them to feel you're appreciative of them, interested in them. Show some empathy and keep them feeling like you care; and you do because you must.

Continue telling them this in any way you can and always keep it personal. You're not talking to a stadium of people. For your purposes you're only speaking to one person, yet all prospects will understand it personally. That's the key to getting customers. It's the process of engagement.

For my own part, I receive emails, phone calls, and messages from marketers who have maintained contact with me over a long time. Most of them offer value along with their messages—tips and information that are valuable to me because they know me and my needs. I know it costs them nothing to offer this, but the point is they stay with me and continue the process of engagement because they're the great marketers who create a pathway for me to come to them.

At some point, it's likely that I'll make a buying decision and purchase their products or services. But it may be quite a while before I do so. The upshot is that I judge those who seem trustworthy and sincere based on their continuous contact.

Those who quit emailing, or contacting me in other ways, are evidently not seeking engagement. They want a quick sale. That tells me a lot about the kind of business philosophy they have, and I'm not inclined to buy from those businesses because I instinctively know they won't back up their products with services after the sale. And I may never hear from them again.

This is one of the big changes in the new marketplace from past methods that are no longer effective. Present your prospects with the process of engagement using emotional intelligence, and you'll attract customers. And you'll keep them. This is one more way your actions put you ahead of your competition.

Keeping customers means you must market, advertise, and sell beyond the message to their emotional motivations. Most any business can get a customer once, but keeping that customer calls for a different set of skills.

It's about how well the people of a business interact with their new customers. You know, speak to them in the language of their perceptions. Help them solve problems. It's what a business does.

It would be very instructive to know how most businesses count prospects (potential customers) who were lost, those who never came back, those who didn't buy because salespeople didn't engage them on an emotional level or seek to understand them and their perceptions of the product.

I'm thinking of many, but not all, car salesmen. My experience has been that they're the most egregious of this kind of thing.

I recall shopping for a convertible. I love them. Sunshine, wind in your hair, the wide-open feeling. Meanwhile, the salesperson was selling me on gas mileage, battery life, and the tires. I wonder how long he lasted as a car salesperson. Does the dealership realize how many buyers he loses rather than how many sales he makes?

This is the true measure of how well your business is serving your customers. It's something every business should strive to know.

Next, learn how two essential questions will greatly improve your marketing strategy and your success in the new marketplace.

IMPROVE YOUR MARKETING STRATEGY BY ANSWERING TWO ESSENTIAL QUESTIONS

1. WHAT IS MY CUSTOMERS' OBJECTIVE?
2. HOW CAN I HELP THEM MEET IT?

Businesses must lead with a marketing-centric (*not* advertising-centric) approach to marketing strategy meaning the advertising originates only from the marketing. Advertising cannot exist alone.

It might surprise you to know how many companies, both big and small, get this wrong. They jump into the marketplace with an advertisement with no plans for its longevity or purpose. Then they go with another advertisement that may or may not match the message of the first. Soon their advertising messages become meaningless. The prospect is left confused with unanswered questions. And an unanswered question is always a negative.

Since it's difficult to overcome existing negatives, assure you've done it right the first time by doing the following before even considering communicating with your prospects.

* Learn what the customer wants, not just what they think about a specific product. Or a competitor's product or brand.
    Why are customers and prospect even considering products in a specific category? What dreams are they trying to achieve? What emotion will be satisfied?
    This should be answered for each type of customer. The answer helps a company discover and define its customer segments. Customer segmentation was described earlier, and it's critical to reaching each kind of customer you acquire within their perceptions of your product or service.

- As for the marketing side of a business, create a customer-experience map charting how your customer experiences the brand. And how your customer experiences competing brands?

  What ways can your company add personalized contacts to create new experiences, new engagements that help deliver what the customer wants?

  The clearest and most effective way to do this is to obtain *customer feedback*, which is *new knowledge* for evaluation and use in improving both your product, your marketing, and your advertising. This is a key element in the creation of your marketing plan.

  For most companies, there should be a customer-response chart for each customer segment. This again involves customer segmentation which is much more important than one might think.

- Serve the customer at each one of these contact points. This is why marketing is so much bigger than just advertising.

  You might discover that customers look to third-party websites and publications to do research before considering your product. By engaging in a content marketing strategy, you could influence more customer decisions *without* buying any more advertising.

  Or you might discover that customers need to personally and tangibly experience your product, but you sell it online. In that case, your marketing strategy might call for investing more budget in customer service and free return shipping thus reducing your budget for advertising. This is what Zappos Shoes did, and these tactics became the most effective aspects of marketing for the brand.

- Serving customers is impossible if you don't first learn what customers want.

  Take free shipping for example.

  When a significant study asked *marketers* how they could improve their customers' shopping experience, providing free shipping was tied for the ninth most popular option at 18 percent.

However, when *consumers* were asked the same question, providing free shipping was by far the most popular response overall at 74 percent.

This is only one example of the many disconnects between what customers value and what marketers value. Understanding how your customers view your business and the way you address their needs is the core element of effective marketing.

- Produce customer-focused advertising, not product-focused advertising.

Product focused advertising does not speak to today's more astute customers. It's the way of the past. The new marketplace is about the way marketers must meet today's customers.

All advertising is personal. We've covered this before, but it bears repeating. A good marketer doesn't advertise as if speaking to an audience or a group of people. A marketer must address the consumer and prospect personally about their personal needs. This is customer-centric or customer-focused advertising. There is no other kind.

What makes one ad better than another? Of course, there are a few basics of a good ad. It grabs the customer's attention. It is placed in the right medium, so the ideal customer sees it.

Yet one of the most important qualities of a good ad is that it uses emotion and empathy to help the customer meet his or her objective. Some ads use creativity to do that. Others use facts and information. But they all directly tie customer's desire to an emotionally beneficial customer need in a quick and compelling way.

It is truly amazing that many marketers don't get this and advertise as if they're in a vacuum. Rest assured, you'll find it's a great benefit for you when you understand your prospects and your marketplace better than your competition.

You'll also find you don't have nearly as much competition as you may have first thought.

FIVE WAYS YOUR BRAIN IS FOOLING YOU

HALLMARKS OF THE BODY'S
MOST MISUNDERSTOOD ORGAN

You've probably found yourself in situations where you felt like either your memory or your perception was somehow distorted. Maybe you'd confess to having bought into a conspiracy theory, entertained a superstition, or even spotted faces in random objects.

If so, don't worry, it's just how the brain work; at least according to Dean Burnett, a neuroscientist at Cardiff University in Wales. In his new book, "The Idiot Brain: A Neuroscientist Explains What Your Head Is Really Up To" (HarperCollins, 2016), he enumerates some of the ways our brains succeed in tripping us up.

His book is an effort to demystify the brain for the average nonscientist. It's an exploration of the quirks and imperfections that are hallmarks of the body's most misunderstood organ.

Familiarity, as we've discussed, can cause us to overlook the obvious. It can also breed contempt. Yet Dr. Burnett doesn't really see it that way.

"I think it's a healthier approach, to (admit) that the brain isn't perfect," says Burnett. "It's brilliant, but it's got plenty of bugs and glitches, and these things affect everyone all the time."

Ultimately, Dr. Burnett hopes that taking an irreverent attitude towards the brain will allow us to be less intimidated by it, improving our understanding by bringing it back down to earth.

"I don't think scientists have the right to tell people that their brains are out of bounds, because what is more our own than the actual grey matter in our heads?" says Burnett.

He goes into considerable detail on a variety of subjects, but here are five things the brain does that Burnett finds amusing and perplexing.

Superstition

The brain is constantly looking for patterns in things, whether or not they actually exist.[8] Consequently, it often leads us to draw connections between disparate events, forming the foundations for many of our superstitions and conspiracy theories.

"The brain doesn't like randomness and uncertainty; it will do everything it can to rule that out," says Burnett. "So, we get things that make no sense, weird theories like, 'Don't throw salt over your shoulder on a Thursday.' 'Don't walk under a ladder.' "Never open an umbrella in a house.' And most of these things tend to be passed along."

No, That's Not Actually Jesus on Your Toast

One particular quirk, similar to the brain's constant attempts to form patterns, is that it's constantly on the lookout for faces. Yes, faces.

"There is a temporal-cortex region of the visual system responsible for recognizing and processing faces," Burnett writes, "so anything that looks a bit like a face will be perceived as a face." Perceptions again.

He says, "We tend to see faces everywhere—in punctuation :-), in bits of toast, clouds, kettles and sinks, cutlery and bits of grass laying on the floor," says Burnett. "It's really harmless, but it can also be quite distracting. It's not a very good use of our time."

Your Memory Is Unreliable and Biased

"People have this idea (about memory) that it's sort of like computer memory. Information goes in, it's stored and then it's retrieved in exactly the same state as it was placed there," says Burnett. The reality, he says, is far more complicated.

"It seems like a seamless memory system, but it's vulnerable to influences," he says. "So, if we ask leading questions, the memory can be altered." The classic example would be of a witness being interrogated or cross-examined by a skilled lawyer in a courtroom.

---

[8] This is the Gestalt theory of psychology

Memory is also informed by our egos. "We tend to adjust memories so that they're more flattering to us, because our self-worth, our self-regard is important to us," says Burnett. "Some people genuinely believe they caught a fish that big, even when they didn't."

Lizard Brain, Meet Neocortex

Burnett talks about our lower order "lizard" brain, (Carl Sagan called it our reptilian brain) that controls our most basic functions such as breathing, balance, and coordination. It's occasionally at odds with the more advanced neocortex.

"You've got these two bits of the brain—one really old, one really new," he says. "One's set in its ways and the other one is thinking and planning and flexible. They don't get on well, but they're both stuck in your head forever, arguing constantly about who does what and how it's done."

A perfect example of this dynamic at play is motion sickness on an airplane, where the brain is receiving conflicting sensory information about whether you're in motion or stationery. "The neocortex knows what's happening—it understands the concept of vehicles and the ability to be in motion without moving your body. But the primitive brain doesn't know that. It can't accept it, and it has no system to be corrected. It just assumes it's been poisoned, so it makes you throw up." It's the reason for the little bags furnished to passengers usually in the seat back in front of you.

Praise Makes Us Feel Pretty Good, But Criticism Makes Us Feel Really Bad

You might notice that you react more strongly to criticism than to praise. According to Burnett, our brains respond differently to each.

"Nice things, such as receiving praise, produce a neurological reaction via the release of oxytocin," he writes, "which makes us experience pleasure, but in a less potent and more fleeting manner."

Being criticized, mocked, or insulted, however, is perceived by the brain as a threat, which induces a stress response and the release of cortisol. "It makes us experience an actual physical reaction that sensitizes us and emphasizes the memory of the event."

UP TO 45 PERCENT OF PEOPLE MAKE THEIR BUYING DECISIONS OUT OF HABIT

AND THEY'RE ALMOST ALWAYS IRRATIONAL DECISIONS

The way we get to work in the morning, the route we take, what we eat for lunch, where we stop to get gas, what kind of gas we buy, what kind of soda we drink. These are all habits.

Understanding how habits function within our brains and within our lives is critical for you to increase the retention of customers, and to keep your customers once you've made them into customers.

We'll look at an example of what this means. The man from Mars is an analogy that constantly comes to my mind about many products, particularly the concept of insurance. I imagine telling a man from Mars to pay me fifty dollars each month, and if he crashes his flying saucer, I'll buy a new one for him. Would that make sense to a man from Mars? I doubt it.

So, imagine for a moment you're a man from Mars studying economics. (That's interesting already.) So, as you're examining our economics, you're presented with these two options:

- Option A: People can make a cup of coffee for 16 to 18 cents in the comfort of their home.
- Option B: They can haul themselves out of bed earlier, stop at Starbucks and pay as much as four or five dollars for a cup of coffee.

Let's assume you're a rational Martian and you expect rational findings, so you're sure that people will choose option A.

But as we Earthlings all know, people don't act rationally. They choose option B. Not everybody, of course, but enough people to generate more than $16 billion in revenue for Starbucks last year. Many people think of this purchase decision as part of daily life.

Categorically, you know it's not a rational economic decision. You have a hard time understanding that every time people make that purchase it's totally irrational. But they do over and over.

So why do people act this way? Well, it's because most people don't make rational decisions, economically or otherwise. Most people are on autopilot following automated habits. And we have to admire Starbucks' marketing department for helping turn a simple cup of coffee into a cheap luxury habit.

It's not just Starbucks, of course. It's the daily newspaper on your driveway. Movie night. And, according to Charles Duhigg,[9] even the mundane act of brushing your teeth is a habit. So, it would serve marketers well to have a basic understanding of the science of habit formation.

It's a well-known factoid that if you as a marketer can get a customer to return to you at least three times, you have a good chance that they've created a habit of doing business with you, albeit, a soft habit. But by their nature, habits tend to become more entrenched the more often the customer reacts to them, that is, returns to your business.

It's also true that habits are at the core of many of the decisions we all make about brands we buy and about consumption.

Think about it. Duhigg says there's no natural state of nature where someone says, "I'm eating a cookie. What I really need right now is a glass of milk." No, that's not a natural state of nature. But that's the power of creating a habit.

It's a habit because somewhere a very clever person figured out how to link cookies and milk in your mind.

The mind is a strange thing. It seeks patterns, the basis of Gestalt psychology. And it thinks according to perceptions, that which it perceives to be already known is reality.

---

[9] Charles Duhigg is a Pulitzer Prize–winning reporter for the *New York Times*. He has researched and written an influential book about the topic —*The Power of Habit: Why We Do What We Do in Life and Business.*

One of the cores of insights about how habits function is the basic finding that every habit has three components. We know this from studies in neurology and psychology.

1. First, a habit has a cue, a trigger event for an automatic behavior to start.
2. Then it becomes a routine, which is the behavior itself.
3. And then there is a reward. The reward is how your brain learns to make that behavior, that pattern, into something automatic. To make it into a habit.

This gives you a powerful tool for trying to understand the cues and rewards that drive how people automatically behave.

A great example of this is video games. When a video game designer designs a new game, the first thing that they decide upon is what the reward schedule is. And that comes from observation. By watching people play their new games (beta testing), they learn when they expect to get something that makes the playing continue because the players think (feel emotionally) it's fun. The decision made by the designers is determined when the players get a reward that can be anticipated by the players, or even if they get a reward they don't anticipate.

Slot machines are designed and operate on the same principle.

There's an insight in this. It's very hard to create a new reward and convince people that they like it. It's much easier to look at what habits already exist naturally and try to piggyback on the rewards that people are giving themselves.

STRATEGY AND TACTICS

THEY MAY NOT BE WHAT YOU THOUGHT

A commonly misunderstood approach to marketing and advertising is to develop a strategy, then use tactics to implement it. While tactics do indeed implement a strategy, this is upside-down thinking, and I'll explain why.

Since analogies of marketing with warfare are the easiest to understand, I'll begin with such a scenario. In a battle for the customer, marketing is essentially warfare. (Don't put too fine a point on it, but many businesses approach the marketplace as if they're in a war.)

Imagine a field commander observing the terrain of the battlefield on which his command will engage the enemy. He sees swamps, he sees hills, roads, and a river, a large lake, and a forest. He knows that his tank corps isn't going to do well in the swamps; they'll become stuck in the mud.

Being a good field commander, he also sees the hills as an advantage for hiding his flanking movements from the enemy. And then there's the open ground where his light artillery and infantry can do the greatest damage in the shortest time by bringing havoc into the middle of the enemy's battle line, hopefully splitting it in two and greatly reducing its threat.

And his heavy artillery can devastate the enemy if it's placed out of sight behind a large hill overlooking the battlefield. The lake and river create natural boundaries; the enemy may cross the river at great peril; or, the enemy is forced to stand and fight risking much higher causalities than they're willing to take.

He sizes up all the information he sees and acknowledges the relative strengths of his army and the enemy's forces.

These are tactics. The weapons and the soldiers are all tactical elements. (Where they're placed and how they're used based on the terrain he must fight upon.) The tactical abilities and the coordination of the tactics themselves used together to engage the enemy become his strategy. This means that a strategy is developed from the tactical elements available and necessary. A strategy is not in any way as important as the tactics. A strategy is only important to assure everyone is on the same page, understands the deployment, and documents it for his superiors so that everyone knows the battle plan.

This is the same need that exists for marketing and advertising strategies. It's to assure that management, marketing, and sales are on the same page. Tactics are the only things that are important. No field commander would plan a strategy and then try to come up with tactics to use without ever seeing the actual battlefield and its terrain. This would practically guarantee his defeat. But it has been done, and battles have been lost. During the civil war, Lincoln remarked that "once more General Burnside has snatched defeat from the jaws of victory." He wasn't amused.

Said another way for market planning and advertising, tactics are those things done to make the cash register ring; the things that motivate the prospect and customer to take action to buy your product or service.

Tactics determine strategy.

Yet I hear this being discussed and planned in a completely opposite way. And I'm sure you have too. I've never understood why it's not instinctive that strategy follows tactics just as it's instinctive that behavior follows belief and perception.

I've been invited to be an observer of marketing and advertising presentations being made to a company's management when the presenter had to read the advertising strategy to the client in order to explain the tactic; a TV spot, magazine ad, website promo, or whatever. And yet this is a tactic to be played out as a part of the overall campaign's strategic purpose. I'm dumbfounded.

If the tactics that create the strategy have been approved by management (and this should have been the first thing done) and everyone is presumably on the same page, then the presentation of a TV spot or brochure or any other aspect of a campaign and the reason why ought to be self-evident.

And here's the thing. If it's not self-evident, then that says the tactic is not correct.

This makes a good case in favor of there being more than one or two management people involved in evaluating and decision making for marketing and advertising. Three to five completely informed and engaged people is even better.

Marketing and advertising decisions will affect the business for months or years to come, so they must match long-term plans and goals identified by management.

THE MARKETING PLAN

THE PROCESS OF EVALUATING YOUR MARKETING

Marketing is a constant accumulation of new data and raw information to study and evaluate everything that must be done to create a product or service and get it to the customer, the end user. It is not a linear effort. It is a dynamic process, alive and organic.

Marketing is not advertising or sales. It is the *direction* of your efforts by the way in which your marketplace must be understood. This requires a full understanding of your product, its perception by prospects, your most probable customer/end user, and the best methods of engaging them.

It is a circular effort – a continuing dynamic with every step, every action, required from research and development through manufacturing and distribution to reaching the prospect/customer with the correct message with the correct media to delivering your product or service to the customer.

It includes understanding the end users' or consumers' satisfaction or dissatisfaction with the product as well as the service by the company. This must include the "why" of such feedback – the reasons why such feedback is given in order to evaluate the findings.

But it doesn't stop here. The evaluation of the consumers' contact and response is the point to begin the process again. This is because one of the most important aspects of good marketing is processing the customers' response as new data, new information, about both the product, your company, and your customer in a continuous effort to update and maintain the best things of your marketing and your product.

With evaluation and existing experience, this new data becomes new knowledge with which to run the process over again, hopefully to gain new methods and new ideas about what you're marketing, how the advertising is working, and how the customer reacts to any adjustment in your tactics.

This new knowledge is a new beginning for the marketing's dynamic continuum. With each cycle of this continuous circular effort we are offered repeated opportunities to enhance both your product and your means for getting and keeping customers.

Creating innovations of the product, service, or sales from the process of evaluation enables your product or service to continually improve. This improvement expands your market by filling a larger market need. And done correctly, this will continually get and keep more customers.

To develop a sound, critical marketing process, we must start into the marketing process with an open, creative attitude and clear objective thinking free of previous notions of identity, image and past beliefs.

We must be extremely focused on the critical issues of the business, of the product, and of the customer segment that has been found through the evaluation process. Examples of critical issues are distribution, finance, production, and availability of resources and raw materials to produce the product.

Focusing on the critical issues also enables us to see the product and service in the ways it is perceived in the minds of prospective customers, and how it compares with other similar products in the marketplace.

Without understanding how your prospects see you; perceive your company and your product or service, there is little chance to credibly and believably form the desired perceptions of your product in the most advantageous position in the prospects' minds.

This is the most important element of marketing. It's what marketing is all about. Please don't take it lightly. Not doing this as well as possible can mean the difference between success and failure. And it is, indeed, the primary reason for both.

CREATING YOUR MARKETING PLAN

STEPS FOR DEVELOPMENT OF
YOUR MARKETING PLAN
FOLLOW THIS LIKE A RECIPE

- Gain as much new knowledge about your marketplace as possible (those who are selling similar things—products or services). How large is your market (that is, how many real potential prospects exist for your specific product or service within the geographic area you can service)? This can be gotten from primary research, studies, feedback and secondary research, and you even find it with Google Analytics.

- Put this newly found knowledge — raw data combined with your existing knowledge and experience. This becomes *new information*, a valuable proprietary body of facts about what you are and how you appear in your marketplace (i.e., product, competition, buyers, and end users).

- Once this *new information* is evaluated, a new need for improving your product or service is always determined. The need or needs are "findings" that then go to your company's research-and-development area for evaluation and feasibility.

- You can expect much *new information* to come out of the investigations by research and development in the form of product or service innovations usually learned from the feedback from your end users to enhance consumer/end user attraction and sales of your product or service. Even something as seemingly insignificant as a longer handle on a broom.

- R&D findings are then evaluated for projecting results in achieving or exceeding sales objectives. This is experiential, of course, and it comes from existing knowledge; i.e., sales statistics, communication contact (media), distributor feedback, end-user feedback, and by direct observation.

- The R&D findings evaluated and approved and guided by your *new information* determine innovations and enhancements incorporated into the product that ought to be included in the message of the sales tactics developed, both internally and externally.

- Sales, revenue and development costs are combined, and objectives are set to match the rationale and purpose of such innovations to create more sales and revenue. Innovation of the original product or service should result in increased sales and revenue. (Some improvements of the product are necessary to maintain value of the product and so may be unrealized or not noticed by your consumers/end users.)

- Determine through research and then evaluate the best tactics by objective to create sales in the most effective way. This is the point at which the means and methods (media, direct sales, point of purchase, in store, etc.) are selected as being the methods best available to get your message to the public – to your prospects and customers.

- Once the tactics that address the objectives are determined, the methods for implementing tactics to create new sales are selected (i.e., after doing the media research that shows you the mediums that will most effectively reach your prospects, your target market).

- Strategy is determined from tactics that are necessary to make sales and create revenue. Strategy means nothing by itself. It's only a statement of purpose of the tactics; a kind of shorthand reference to the combined tactics. Everything done must be consistent with the tactics needed to make sales, create new customers, and keep existing customers.

- Implement the tactics and carefully monitor the results. Match every objective achieved with the tactic that was used to achieve it. This is vital for any objective assessment of the tactics.

- Continually evaluate media, outside sales efforts, and any other methods of attaining your objectives. Adjust tactics as necessary based on which are performing best in attaining the objectives.

- Develop and implement an effective quantitative means for customer/ end user feedback of their satisfaction with the product, the real or perceived value of the product innovations, and which tactics are most effective. The most critical piece of knowledge you must learn from the feedback is "what are the perceptions of the product and of your company that are held by the customer, and what can be done to improve them?" Customer satisfaction is the measure of the marketing effort.

- Evaluate results of the feedback and put them back as "new information" and begin the process all over again. This process is constantly and consistently repeated to inform you, the company, where you are in the marketplace, what your customers think, what are their perceptions, what innovations are needed to improve sales, and most importantly, are you losing customers or gaining them? The big takeaway here is that you must know beyond doubt what your customers are feeling and whether they're remaining to be customers. Secondarily, the measure of new customers will reveal whether your marketing is successful; i.e., you're always seeking new customers.
- **Memo** about the Longer Term
- There are only *two* ways to increase market share if you're in a mature (saturated) market:

  1. Product proliferation; i.e., increased distribution
  2. Product innovation; to make the product distinctive from your competition. This can be as simple as a revised but still familiar label. Even adding the words "new" or "improved" on your label is an innovation. (Caveat: Never change your name, your logo, or your basic label design. Doing any of these will make you invisible.)

That these are your only two options for growth should not be thought of as a limitation. We all know what Steve Jobs did with Apple and made it the largest company in the world.

Jobs claims to have never done a marketing or feasibility study. He said he already knew what people wanted, but since there was nothing else like it in the world, people (future customers) didn't know of it, and so couldn't explain what they wanted. Therefore, he said, a feasibility study was worthless.

There are very few people of Steve Jobs' caliber in the world, but still, innovation and proliferation are the very best ways of getting new customers and keeping them. It amounts to continually making your product better (and telling everyone about it) and increasing its distribution, it's availability to the consumer. Jobs did this with remarkable clarity and near omniscience. He's an example of why some people are known as geniuses.

Strive to continually do these two things. They're simply the best and most enduring way to get and keep more and more customers. To grow.

Apple has done this each year with their telephone (iPhone), a simple thing on the surface, but they were the first in the market with anything as totally new and unique as the iPhone.

Being first in the marketplace is a very powerful thing because it automatically made Apple the market leader. Now each year their customers have come to expect another innovation. They have been trained to expect it, and they stand in lines for days to give Apple their money for the latest innovation of the iPhone regardless of the price. Keep that in mind.

Apple is constantly innovating every product they market. So much so that my seven-year old Apple Macintosh is so out of date it doesn't accept the newest versions of its own operating system. Obsolescence of an older version of your product is another source of revenue, so long as you keep your customers. Automobile companies have gotten this down to a science as have computer companies.

However, not constantly improving the quality of their product is the grand mistake that Detroit automakers made and continue to make.

They aren't alone. We can say the same of several industry segments including banking, airlines, hotels, railroads, and shopping malls, among others. A few improvements, but no overarching innovations. Not surprisingly, these industry segments are presently experiencing their market limitations. And some are in decline.

With today's new management systems, technologies, and product innovations, instant communications, and faster paced marketing, the world is passing them by.

I wonder if they even know it.

CUSTOMER-PROSPECT IDENTIFICATION FINDING OUT WHO YOUR CUSTOMERS ARE

HOW TO KNOW YOUR CUSTOMER EVEN BETTER

Increasing ways of identifying your customers and understanding them even better is hugely important. It outweighs other needs by far.

Just because I waited until this point to tell you about it does not mean it's less important. It's because most people aren't ready to think about this or to understand it until they have a grasp of their market and marketing process. You'll see what I mean when we get into it.

- Who are your prospects and customers?
- Why are they prospects and customers?
- And what do you learn from knowing this? And how?

We learn these from customer-prospect identification. This is crucially important to know. If you've worked through your marketing plan, then this is the next thing to know. Customer-prospect identification is super-critical to knowing your customers, and it only consists of two elements or parts:

1. Customer Segmentation
2. Predictive Modeling of Customer Segments

Some misunderstand this process. These terms are not to be used interchangeably. They're very different and support different business-marketing objectives

Customer Segmentation

Customer segmentation is the practice of identifying and classifying your existing customer base into distinct groups or *market segments.* It's the most important action one can take in defining their marketplace and its size. And it proves that not everyone sees things the same way, or for the same reason.

Market segmentation is the way you identify significant variances in your total customer group. So, any variance defines a new customer segment. Segmenting your target group is the most important thing for your marketing. So, you must segment your market group down to the smallest possible segment for the best results.

You must always be segmenting and segmenting again and again, so you hone your position and message to a razor edge for each segment, since each segment will have subtle but distinct needs. Then do the same with your prospects in the same segment because prospective customers in each segment will be similar.

Doing marketing well means you'll always be reaching out and drawing in your best prospects and existing customers; those who have the greatest proclivity to buy your offering. Then you can focus your message to each segment with no wasted advertising efforts, a rifle shot instead of a shotgun (which never works).

The most basic customer segments are the following:

- demographic
- psychographic

This separation of prospects and customers into unique groups is based on existing knowledge of customer behavior, motives, and experience, plus information and new knowledge gained by research.

Segmentation should be done again and again from customer feedback. This constant updating is one of the major qualifiers of your market, so it becomes new information to be processed with existing knowledge and experience again and again to refine your offering to its most desirable perception for your market—your customers and prospects.

Note: For the most part, your message to your customers and prospects are similar. Depending on your product, it's probable that the message is the same. Don't make the mistake of believing that your message to existing customers will remain top-of-mind forever.

- Demographics
  Age, race, education, marital status, income, regions of the country, and whether they're urban, suburban, or rural.
  Demographic studies can be carried out as far as you wish, and your group becomes smaller as more qualifiers are added. This is extreme segmentation based on demographics.
  Extreme segmentation differs in purpose and result from segmenting generally, as has been discussed. I only advise extreme segmentation if you're selling highly individualistic, boutique kinds of products, and when and if only a very few have the proclivity to buy for reasons you've found to be the primary motivator and benefit to the buyer.

- Psychographics (Many Are Linked to Elements of Demographics)
  Life-stage characteristics are generally found in these categories: youth, career building, attainment, age-based behavior – young, middle age, older, as well as lifestyle, preferences and interests.
  Behaviors identified by self-reported or secondary research about product/service preferences, needs and attitudes observed from tracking customer purchases and product usage.
  This is an important psychographic, and it should only come from your company's findings from feed-back of users and customer. Some of this is information that can be purchased, but purchased information is not as specific and never as good as your own findings.
  Insights gained from segmentation identify unique characteristics of a customer group or market segment. Some companies may have as few as three unique segments, while other companies require as many as twenty segments to satisfy their market/sales needs. How many you determine is needed depends on your findings from feed-back from customers about your product or service.

Predictive Modeling

Predictive modeling is done after segmenting. It's the practice of forecasting future customer behaviors and propensities and assigning a score or ranking to each customer segment that it depicts (i.e., prediction of their anticipated actions).

Identify and isolate customer characteristics that are highly correlated with your own objectives and outcomes. These are key to defining your tactics and can eventually revise the way you set up your strategy because strategy is derived from your most effective tactics.

- In segmentation, a critical consideration is how many segments.
- In predictive modeling, a critical consideration is how many different models will be required or necessary *within* a segment.

A single segmentation scheme can sometimes be applied across all the areas—segment, target group, and position — while predictive models are typically developed for a very specific purpose.

For example, a company may develop several customer purchase propensity models for each of its key products.

The insights gained from each of the models can then be used independently or collectively to shape the tactics for targeting in product cross-sell campaigns.

Cross-sell and up-sell campaigns are derived from your ability to find like kinds of interests by customers for yet another product offering. "Do you want fries with that?" is a well-known up sell.

If you've ever used Amazon.com to buy a book, then you're aware of this tactic. Amazon has mastered it. The website's integral algorithms do this automatically. If you buy a book, a small text line appears that states, "Others who have purchased this book also purchased these books." It cleverly keeps you within the book subject genre in which you have made your purchase and is attractive to your propensity to make similar purchases.

No one can top Amazon for sales and tracking. Amazon is run by a technology one might call robotics. It's really a gigantic search engine in which you can find practically anything you want. But don't try to copy

Amazon's business model. It's unduplicatable and hugely expensive; that's why it's so successful.

But you can duplicate this cross sell, or up sell, by merely keeping track of customer purchases and following up with them.

I've helped many clients set up Excel or similar spreadsheets as data bases to track customers. It can be done by using product numbers, or other identification codes of a product, then simply entering it as a sale is made. This then goes directly to a data base automatically.

(Note: Wal-Mart uses a larger version of this for inventory control and it's automated to the extent that products showing up as low on inventory are automatically re-ordered.)

DEAR READER

I've written this book to be used as a tool by any small business.

Marketing is a broad, complex subject, which takes a considerable amount of information to make sense, to be understandable, and to be useable.

Any of the concepts, ideas, and information I've explored here can be discussed and expanded upon at great length. But if I'd written everything that can be known and used in marketing, this book would be hundreds of pages long, and I'd probably still be writing it. This would be self-defeating because you'd think twice about reading it. We all seem to be running fast to stay ahead of our work and the things we want to do. So, it would make little sense to write a book few people will ever read.

I very much appreciate your having read this book. I hope I've helped you in your marketing efforts without causing cognitive overload. I hope you've gained some insights and actionable knowledge about small business's marketing for any product or service you're selling in the marketplace.

I look forward to hearing your comments about this book or about marketing that you may wish to make to me personally.

Contact me by email at: doug@douglaskellymarketing.com.

I encourage you to read my blog: www.douglaskellymarketing.com and leave a comment. My purpose is to help small businesses succeed in their marketplaces. Everyone's ideas and concepts add to the overall benefit to all marketers. The more who participate the better for all of us who read it.

NOW, A LITTLE ABOUT MYSELF

I began my career with one of the largest marketing and advertising firms in the nation. These people were very good at what they did, and so I was able to learn a lot about the craft of marketing from the inside out.

Several years later, I opened my own business. And once fully established, I became a member of AAAA (American Association of Advertising Agencies).

I'm proud of my company's membership in this organization because only 8 percent of all advertising agencies are members, yet they place more than 92 percent of all advertising.

And here's the thing: An advertising agency can't just write a check and become a member as one can with most trade associations. There is a rigorous process by which the AAAA audits the agency's books and contacts your competitors and vendors to confirm that the agency conducts itself with the highest ethical standards and practices. Then, if these elements are found to be satisfactory, the agency is nominated and voted on by local and national member agencies to allow membership in the AAAA. So, not every applicant becomes a member.

Once a member, AAAA is a wonderfully vast resource for agency operations, industry best practices, knowledge of specific markets, as well as being a source for secondary research in any category.

I operated my advertising and marketing firm for more than 35-years. During this time, my clients were regional, national, and international businesses in more than eighty product and service categories with nearly every conceivable need.

Because of my natural curiosity, it was a sheer joy. I enjoyed it immensely because I am fascinated by the psychology of the ways people act and react to stimulus. And I'm continually curious about all the ways it occurs. It's the most enjoyable way I could have lived my life during those thirty-five years or so.

Printed in the United States
By Bookmasters